THE ORIENTAL RUG

THE ORIENTAL RUG

LUCIANO COEN
and
LOUISE DUNCAN

HARPER & ROW, PUBLISHERS
NEW YORK, HAGERSTOWN, SAN FRANCISCO, LONDON

Photographs on pages 3, 16, 24, and 28 courtesy of
Photo Researchers, Inc.

Sundry rug patterns courtesy of Office du Livre,
Fribourg, Switzerland.

Endpaper map and various rug patterns drawn by
John Woodford Rapp, Jr.

First published in Canada by Fitzhenry & Whiteside Limited,
Toronto.

FIRST EDITION

Designed by Lydia Link

Manufactured by Chanticleer, Inc.

Library of Congress Cataloging in Publication Data

Coen, Luciano.
  The oriental rug.
  Bibliography: p.
  Includes index.
  1. Rugs, Oriental. I. Duncan, Louise,
joint author. II. Title.
NK2808.C55 1978   746.7′5   76–5119
ISBN 0–06–010824–X

78 79 80 81 82 10 9 8 7 6 5 4 3 2 1

Dedicated with love to

MRS. VIRGINIA HILU
and
SIG. MONI PONTREMOLI

CONTENTS

PLATES

PERSIA

TURKEY

THE CAUCASUS

CENTRAL ASIA

CHINA

PREFACE

As a lifelong private collector who has recently elected to join the "ill gender" of rug dealers, I feel entitled to indicate the merits of the many—fortunately—dealers who operate as you wish them to, up to the standards of professional ethics. As a dealer who is in love with Oriental rugs, I may also be allowed to state that there are certain customer ethics that do not contemplate arrogance, presumption, and poor taste as a substitute for lack of knowledge. The field of Oriental rugs is vast, mysterious, and intriguing. Something new is to be learned by all of us from the apparently most insignificant Oriental mat. Let us walk hand in hand, confidently. Let us meet Oriental rugs in their native lands. Let us get to know them and enjoy their company as the company of our warmest friends.

Luciano Coen

Rome, Italy
1977

ACKNOWLEDGMENTS

The rugs illustrated (other than Mr. Coen's) are in the collections of Mr. Vojtech Blau, New York, Mr. D. Schatzman, Berne, Switzerland, and Dr. Christiano Napoleone, Pescara, Italy.

We wish to thank Mrs. Harriet Stanton, New York, Mr. Thomas Lipscomb, New York, Mr. Fred Moheban, New York; Miss Paulette Lucks, New York; and Mr. Bill Emery, Johannesburg, South Africa, for their kind assistance.

INTRODUCTION

IT IS PROBABLY FAIR to say that the best Oriental rugs have already been woven. Because the character and worth of these rugs has changed so drastically in the last half-century, it is more important than ever to know the various traditions that gave birth to such a cultural manifestation as well as whatever inherent value the design carries. As in wine growing, there are good years and bad years, a good Sarouk and a bad Sarouk. The differences between rugs could be compared to the differences among the great chateaux. Obvious benefits accrue to the owner from knowing these differences and from nurturing them as they age. And, like the wine merchant, the rug dealer can be one's best friend.

A good Oriental rug has the qualities one looks for in a work of art and evokes the same response in the viewer. From an aesthetic point of view, the designs are infinitely curious, the colors fantastic, the work required stupendous. For hundreds of years Oriental rugs have been collected by every advanced civilization in the world. Beginning with the simple universal designs anthropologists find nomadic tribes weaving into early articles of the most utilitarian nature, Oriental rugs have evolved into a complex art form.

Oriental rugs have always been bought in the West because they add life and an exotic touch to a room. They are thought to be a good investment when the color improves with age (because it was made from vegetable dyes) and when they wear well (meaning, in this context, several hundred years). Even then, the resale value depends on the condition of the rug.

As an art or a craft, weaving is rather interesting to consider. Painters can return to their work ten years after they began and change what they have done, and indeed there are many stories of Picasso adding a touch after a dècade or of an artist arriving at a dinner party with his paints to change a picture he has wanted to alter for some time. But weaving is a no-smudge medium. It is even more difficult to take a knot out than it is to form one. Rodin did hundreds of drawings throughout his career to learn about the tensions in the human body, but a sketch of a rug before it is knotted can only approximate the colors that the dye creates in the yarn and the harmonies that result in the whole. While a painter may make a sketch on a menu and later see it hung in the Metropolitan Museum, a room-sized rug takes three or four weavers over a year to make, and a saddle rug takes six months of hard work on a movable loom. An artist may draw a perfect curved line in the glance of an eye, but putting a curved line into a knotted rug, working from row to row, is a technique that takes years to learn and months to execute. It is interesting to look at one knot, then the whole rug, and try to imagine the astonishing organizational acumen that went into its knotting.

People speak in awe of a rug that has 250 knots per square inch, and there is no question that the more thickly knotted the rug, the more supple and strong it is, and usually the more subtle its design. From a technical standpoint, the colors are as remarkable as the knotting. "Vegetable" dyes are taken from berries, insects, or plants, and only recently have synthetic dyes begun to approach their quality. Vegetable colors dye unevenly for the simplest of reasons: When a hank of yarn is dipped in a vat of dye and hung to dry, the threads on top dry first and the ones on the bottom, heavy with liquid, dry last and have the most concentrated color. The result is magnificent. When one looks closely at a patch of red in an Oriental rug, flecks of rose, carmine, vermilion, and orange may be seen. From a distance these blend into a brilliant, true color. Unforunately, with the introduction of ready-made aniline dyes in the 1860s the days of vegetable dye were numbered. To be sure, aniline dyes had a certain charm when a rug was first completed, but they faded and discolored very quickly, and today many of these rugs are unusable. One of the best characteristics of an Oriental rug, and part of its mystique, is the idea that it lasts longer than a lifetime and even grows more beautiful with age. This is often true when natural dyes are used.

A dealer in fine rugs is more likely to be found in a great Western city that prides itself on its cosmopolitan taste than in a rug bazaar in Teheran or Istanbul. For two centuries the West has absorbed all the Oriental rugs it could buy, but now that the Middle Eastern states are becoming more affluent they are repatriating their own art treasures. This turn has already had a substantial effect on the market. But whatever the influence on the market, first and last one's reaction to an Oriental rug is subjective and personal. There is no right or wrong in taste. Cost depends on popularity. The words one reads or hears are unimportant compared with what the eyes and heart say in response to a rug as a work of art.

One of the difficulties of learning about Oriental rugs is that most of the sources concerning their early existence are in Arabic. As Arabic suffers inordinately from translation, it is wise to remember the subtleties of language and ideas while reading about the Islamic world. In reverse, we in the West have named these rugs "Oriental." The word comes from the Latin verb *oriri,* to rise; hence, the lands where the sun rises. The general term *Orient* means "the East." To a Westerner it implies also the exotic connotations of Eastern culture. But to a Persian the East is China, and to the Chinese the East is in the Pacific. What they weave is familiar to them, part of a heritage centuries long, and we are the strangers who live thousands of miles away. In one sense, this means that to a European or American every rug made in the East is an "Oriental" rug.

More specifically, an Oriental rug comes from what is now Turkey, Iran, the Caucasus, Central Asia, India, and China. Among the better-known rugs in the West are Oushaks, Bergamas, Kashans, Kirmans, Tabrizes, Sarouks, Kazaks, "Bokharas," Agras, and Pekings. Although their origins may be separated by thousands of miles, their many common cultural and thematic roots unite them in feeling. Poverty and a nomadic life style are found in every country where Oriental rugs are woven. The Islamic tradition suffused all with its brilliant surface decoration, and the symbolic motifs and decorative conventions of each region traveled from country to country, to be transfigured by each new people who used them. The dragon motif, for example, found in the earliest fragments of Persian rugs, was originally an emblem for the Chinese emperor. Eventually it traveled to the Caucasus and thence to Turkey and Asia Minor. The dragon was even found on an Egyptian tapestry dated before the birth of Christ.

Cultural influences were spread through the Middle East by war as well as mere proximity. Darius the First, Alexander the Great, Kubla Khan, and Tamerlane, the Mongolian who came down from the north and subjugated huge areas, were unifying forces in their short-lived attempts at colonization. What is seen under stress is remembered. When the symbols of the foreign ruler became familiar, the captive state would begin to use them as its own.

Photograph by Tom McHugh

Nomadic weaver. This member of one of the few remaining nomadic tribes, the Kashgai of Iran, weaves under the sun on a very crude horizontal loom.

Obviously, this huge region contained many cultural differences. In Iran and India rich, opulent courts encouraged their weavers to supply them with coverings of the most luxurious nature; in China, Confucian thought ruled what is considered to have been the world's most advanced early civilization for centuries; and in the Caucasus there were snowy mountains so filled with light that they were more evocative than any rug ever knotted.

Rugs were quite small in the beginning, woven on portable hand looms easily carried by horse, camel, or donkey. For generations a nomadic family would carry a record of its pattern on what looks to the uninitiated eye like a handful of kindling tattooed with notches and festooned with loops of crude, varicolored yarn. This tradition preserved the family's self-consciousness and hung its tents with the ambiance of its own name. The wealth of a tribal chieftain was calculated in terms of the rugs he owned; special rugs were woven for the bride, others spread on the sand for a caucus of sheikhs. So to its weavers an Oriental rug had many meanings: heritage, time, money, and the representation of an inner life that only its creator could appreciate.

But as the nomadic groups united to build organized societies, considerably larger rugs, often palace rugs, developed in a different style. While the smaller rugs usually feature angular designs, the large ones are veritable gardens of the utmost delicacy. These are the two classic styles of Oriental rugs; in the same rug bazaar one can find an irregular little Kazak woven in a clashing geometric design, with a primitive vigor and a boldness that would impress the most avant-garde modern sculptor, alongside a huge Tabriz of such subtle hues and flowery arabesques that it would appeal to exquisitely refined taste, evoking elegance with every stylized blossom.

Rugs have many sizes and shapes, reflecting the variety of reasons for which they were woven. There are cushions, saddle rugs, prayer rugs, hearth rugs, pillar rugs, wedding rugs, rugs to a benefactor, and rugs to Allah. They are woven in a number of materials—silks and metallic threads as well as wool and cotton. The details of weaving have just as many variations—there are sculptured rugs, pileless rugs, rugs with a fringe underneath and a flat surface on top, and selvages and warp ends finished and knotted in every conceivable design from barber stripes to latticework.

Some of the earliest indications of culture ever found have been tapestry and rug fragments. The Pasyrik rug, which dates from the fifth century B.C., was found on the Mongolian border of Russia. In ancient literature rugs were mentioned by many writers, including Pliny, Xenophon, and Athenaeus. Identified from the time of Cyrus the Great in the sixth century B.C., they were usually cited as examples of the wealth of Babylon and Persia, the cultural and political rulers of the Middle East. A seventh-century A.D. manuscript describes a carpet that Khusrau II placed in the Palace of Ctesiphon. Its purpose was to remind the king of spring during the cold months of winter. It was woven of gold and silver thread and covered with gems on a field depicting a garden with canals, birds, trees, and flowers. It is said to have been so large that it was divided among the conquerers of the palace.

Since the Crusades, Oriental rugs have been imported into the West, searched out with the same enthusiasm as spices and silks. The great caravan routes of the Middle Ages passed through the most productive rug regions of Asia, and thus Western agents became knowledgeable in what to collect and why. Oddly enough, it is because of the amber trade that we know the extent and influence of these ancient trade routes. Rather than the precious stone it was thought to be at the time, amber is fossilized resin from the lower Baltic region. Because of its still-changing chemical composition, it may be carbon-tested for age. Amber beads are found all along the trade routes, where they fell from jouncing saddlebags, making it possible not only to date them but also track the trade routes.

In many of the great paintings of the Italian Renaissance and the Flemish masters Turkish rugs are represented—not primitive mats but gorgeous, complex coverings —indicating their role as a status symbol in the society of the period. Lotto and Holbein became so associated with certain types of rugs they depicted that in the trade there is a type of rug named after each. "Oriental" rugs were particularly well suited to the taste of the Renaissance, where individuality with balance was so highly prized, because each one was unique—in color, design, and style. By contrast, the rugs made in our time are standardized, even though many of them are hand woven, resulting in even higher prices for the antiques. Rug weaving is acknowledged to have reached its peak in the sixteenth century, when the most splendid garden and hunting rugs in existence were woven.

Not surprisingly, since the Crusades Western taste has influenced the color and design of Oriental rugs, as rugs that were not made for native family use were woven for courts and for the Western market. For over a century weaving was the main source of foreign income and trade in Turkey and Iran, and even today a large portion of their factory rugs are designed for European and American consumption.

In their native setting, the early palace rugs were designed to be part of a group. Usually a large rug was placed between two runners, which might have been a pair but did not "match" the large one in the center. Across the top was a third carpet called a *kellegi*, rectangular but of considerably larger width than the runners. The cumulative effect of the rhythm and vitality and color surging toward the view from the rugs, which look almost as if they have been piled on top of each other, is very powerful, particularly when one is sitting on them. (Until recent trends toward Westernization, there was very little furniture, only a few cushions and the rugs.) In the tents of the nomads, rugs were not only placed on the ground but also hung around the sides as protection against the wind. In the West, by contrast, we isolate each rug on the floor to show off its properties.

An acceptance of the differences in aesthetic viewpoint between the East and the West is essential to the enjoyment of their art. The rugs are like nothing made in the West, their forms at first mysterious, if not totally inimical to Western art. The phrase that best describes the feeling the critic has is that a Western artist would simply never think to organize the design elements as iconography in the way the Eastern artist has. Nor would a Western artist even use the same alphabet of elements. In the East there are dragons, phoenixes, cloudbands, and the hand of God, literally painted on the piece; in the West, the Madonna and Child.

In viewing any "oriental" art it is important to have a perspective on these differences, to know what stylistic considerations must be taken into account, and how these factors should be interpreted. First, nothing like these rugs would ever be woven in America, in France, or even in Spain, where at one time a thriving rug industry was set up and perpetuated by Muslims who had come from much farther East. But usually the specific elements of the Eastern difference from the West are difficult to pinpoint, in part because the appeal of art is so universal that it works against any definition of differences. However, in this case the look is so recognizable that it would seem as if all Oriental rugs were off the same bolt and one had only to unroll it to a certain place to find a particular rug. They all appear to be variations on a theme. By contrast, Western rug weaving is not homogeneous. English rugs are dissimilar from French or Spanish, and in America pile weaving of this quality does not exist.

As previously mentioned, the two types of Oriental rugs, the flowery Persian and the geometric Caucasian and Turkish, feed into each other as far as their design elements go, transmuting the same symbols by the alchemy of a weaver's perception into what could be called the hard version and the soft version of their common motifs. Both types are highly stylized. One is graceful, based on flowers, delicate and light, while the other is noisy, jarring, and calls attention to itself. One is filled with curls and swirls and arabesques, the other with angles and patterns of the same swirls, transformed by the hard edge and the snowflake. A once-round medallion is now a polygon or an octagon.

In view of the fact that the designs are based on flowers and the garden and certain common religious symbols, it would be natural to assume that these are immediately recognizable in the rugs. Although one can see whatever flowers are in the rugs, the recognition stops there. The West has only broken away from representational art in the past 100 years, but in the East art has been stylized, or abstracted, for centuries. In Persian miniatures and Chinese paintings, for example, one sees a stylization of reality, not an attempt to duplicate its appearance on a flat surface.

Pictorially speaking, an Oriental rug never imparts a feeling of perspective. While there may be flowers of many different sizes on the same carpet, none is ever behind another or spatially anterior to it. A medallion may dominate a design, and consequently the flowers in the field may be used as "background"; but they are always on the same plane. Although this is characteristic of primitive art, in this case it may be seen as sophisticated, for after all a floor covering is meant to embellish a flat surface and not to give one the feeling of being about to step into a hole. The flowers in a rug are like the flowers in a painting by Henri Rousseau—flat, stylized, and unrealistic in their dimensions.

While Oriental art is ultimately nonrepresentational, it is not free in the same way as Western "free" or abstract art. Eastern designs are almost always prototypes, and one of the most fascinating approaches to the rugs is to be aware of the differences and idiosyncracies of the individual rug within these fairly rigid limitations. The design in an Oriental rug can usually be worked out mathematically, as there is almost always an axis that cuts through a series of triangles. The ratio of the intersecting lines is one to two, three, or four. Often the basic design of a rug type is identical

Mihrab. This is the arch where the Muslim prays five times a day. Often small, portable rugs are woven simulating this shape for the religious enthusiast to pray on when he is unable to go to the mosque. This particular arch is in the Madrasa Imami in Ispahan. Often prayer arches are decorated with a hanging lamp and two standing candelabra, which are depicted in prayer rugs.

Although the Madrasa Imami is dated 1354, the writing styles would indicate that it was completed over a period of time. The square outside band of tiles contains modern Arabic script, as does the square cartouche on the back wall of the prayer niche itself. The delineated arch, however, is decorated with *kufic* script on pale tiles. *Kufic* is older, more restrained than the current writing style, and considered by many to be more decorative. It has furnished the border designs for many Caucasian rugs as well as the oft-mentioned "Holbein" rugs.

Surrounding the cartouche on the wall of the niche are tiles designed and worked into medallions. It is evident that the tiles are interchangeable. Aside from the mathematical dexterity that has gone into this design, its changing focus is a tribute to the sophistication of the artist. Of course, the mosque was erected before the zenith of the Persian book.

On the outside face above the arch, the white lines, which are arabesque, give an indication of what complexity that form eventually reached.

but the secondary offshoots are varied. Since the proportions are so often discovered to be based on a series of triangles, a repeated medallion design has the appearance of ending at the border in what seems to be half of a medallion. To the weaver it is not half a medallion but a complete triangle. Variation and individuality were expressed within fairly rigid limitations.

Aside from the motifs, color is used in a manner totally inimical to Western tradition. At first when one looks at an Oriental rug it appears that every color in the spectrum has been thrown in at random, crowded beside each other in little bits and pieces. As we know it, there is no color organization, there are no highlights and no gradations. An Oriental rug is somewhat like a late medieval stained-glass window in its use of color, the difference in a window being the strong black outline around each piece of glass lent by the lead that fitted it. Somehow the panoply of colors in a good rug works harmoniously, emerging as one of its strongest points. When one looks at a rug for a long period, one discovers that the colors do indeed have a plan. (Stepping away from a rug in order to look at it from a distance is not the answer, for no larger scheme is revealed.) The harmony is born out of the weaver's own traditions, and to understand it one must try to see the way the weaver does. With enough concentration the harmony becomes evident. The weaver's use of color is based on contrast, while ours is based on similarity or artifice. In a Rembrandt, the lamp acts as a focal point and demonstrates the artist's expertise in an overall scheme that is generally dark against dark, but in an Oriental rug a small red shape is flush against an equally small blue or yellow one, all the colors having the same degree of brightness. There are no shadows, only an occasional echo. Rarely does one find differentiation in tone or gradations of the same color.

This plethora of colors is one method of augmenting the complexity of design. "Filled" hardly describes the pattern of an Oriental rug. The designs are dense and complex, giving the impression of being tightly fitted together on the surface. When this is not well done it appears "busy," as do the many colors when they are not successfully blended together, but when it is a success it is a masterpiece.

An Oriental rug is exotic, then, and recognizably so, for several reasons: symbols, abstraction, the use of color, and density of surface design—the classic characteristics of nonplastic Islamic art. Islamic art, like most art movements as well as many of the great religions, social changes, and civilizations, began with an idea. In this case it was an expression of faith. Muhammed was born in Arabia, but his religion spread from Western China to Spain, as far north as the Caucasus and as far south as the Sahara Desert. The religion itself includes certain Christian and Judaic ideas, such as divine omnipotence, paradise, and a preordained fate, but its essence is contained in five laws that are quotidian rather than philosophical, more earthward than heavenward. One thing these laws make clear is that Muhammed knew the strength of discipline and habit. The first rule is the recognition that there is one God and that his apostle is Muhammed. Second, five prayers are given at the same time each day in the same manner, wherever the worshiper may be. Third, charity is in the form of alms. Fourth, fasting is observed during the month of Ramadan between sunup and sundown. Fifth, a pilgrimage must be made to Mecca during one's lifetime. Ancillary to these rules is that the five prayers are preferably given in a mosque but in any case must be given in a clean place, and many people carry prayer rugs with them for this purpose. The most common motif in the prayer rug depicts the *mihrab,* or altar, in a mosque, such as the illustration. Mecca is the birthplace of Muhammed, and again, many rugs, both saddle rugs and prayer rugs, are woven just for the pilgrimage.

Muhammed preached what he had learned from a book that Gabriel had brought him. What he said was in turn written in the Koran (recitation). The Koran, one of the most beautiful texts in history, is divided into 114 chapters. Because it is so highly revered in the Arab world and is in fact considered to exist only in Arabic, and because so few people knew how to read when it was written, calligraphy has also played a large part in the decorative arts of the Islamic world. As in China, the Muslim calligrapher is a respected artist enjoying a position of high esteem. Not surprisingly, then, some of the rugs are decorated with Islamic writing. *Kufic,* the oldest style of writing, is somewhat stiff and formal, resembling the typical Chinese design. At one point *kufic* was decorated to such an extent that the tops of the letters were connected by straight-line designs similar to the endless knot of China. As a matter of fact, the attenuation of the letters with extended designs became the style after the Mongol invasion in the thirteenth century. The other kind of Arabic script, which we are more accustomed to seeing, is called *nashki.* These flowing letters are connected by curls and swirls that one will see decorating the *mihrab* in a prayer rug, dedicating the rug to a patron, or stating an old saying or a religious message on the border.

Not surprisingly, the book became one of the major art forms in Persia, and it is surmised that the tradition of using the medallion as one of the major units of design developed from the decoration of books. The medallion was explored further by the widespread use of tiles, in which it was refined to expose the many niceties that are so often seen today.

Islamic art is not religious art per se. The weavers pray for Allah's blessing before beginning a rug and dedicate the best ones to him, but there is no religious iconography, the theory being that an image would give humans a false impression of their own importance. Similarly, each work must be irregular in some respect to show that nothing is perfect but Allah. Because of these strictures, the focus is on the external. The surface of a bowl, painting, or rug is generally covered with design. Typically, the design is an overall pattern without a dominant element. But because of its irregularity and color it is never monotonous and rarely boring.

Of all the Islamic motifs, the arabesque is used more than any other in all the artistic media. It is varied so extensively that books have been written about it. As a design, it is derived from, or a free interpretation of, the acanthus, a prickly herb indigenous to Mediterranean countries. The pattern was developed in Egypt as far back as 1000 A.D. The leaf itself has several serrated sections on either side of the spine, and in the arabesque it appears to be split from a continuous stem. An arabesque can be as simple as a curved line with a loop in it, but usually it is a rich series of curves that twine around each other, knot together, separate, and meet at intervals by being intersected with leaves. Often it seems as though one leaf grows

Acanthus leaves

9

out of another in an endless pattern, and it is so; but at the same time, when all the knotting and bunching and curving has been done, it will almost always have developed into a homogeneous design with no end that goes around the medallion in the center of the rug. As an all-over design, not only can it have great rhythm and vitality but it has a unifying effect on the pattern of the whole rug.

Other important influences, but of a completely different nature, are geographic considerations. The major rug-producing areas are all within the latitude between 25 and 45 degrees north. One theory suggests that north of this, fur was so abundant it was used as warm coverings for the tents of nomadic peoples, but it was scarce enough in the rug-producing areas to have caused the herdsmen to create a synthetic fur. South of this latitude rushes were woven into mats as much to keep the floors cool in the very hot summers as to provide heat in the light winters. The only rug-weaving areas where the cold could be said to be really invigorating were the Caucasus and China. There are river valleys through Persia and some forest areas, but in most of the country the colors of the terrain are so bleached by the sun that in contrast to the rugs they are relatively neutral. What is crucial about the terrain as an influence on the design is that there was very little water or vegetation, but miles of desert, rocky steppes, and rugged, sparsely covered mountains. To a Westerner a garden is a place of flowers and color, but to a Persian it is a place where there is a pool of water. As evidence of the scarcity and value of water, one of the earliest art forms in this region was the bowl. Just as a native hides under layers of clothing for protection from the heat of the day and the cold of the night, a garden hides its treasure of water behind a wall and covers it with trees. The trees are protection; the water, life. To a Persian, the flowers in a rug mean water, and rug after rug is covered with thick patterns of flowers of every kind stylized in every possible way, scattered, in vases, as arabesques, lined up and twined together in borders, used as a focus and a background, and woven in every color and in silk, wool, cotton, gold, and silver. The Persian word for walled garden means "paradise."

For centuries, weaving was a family project in nomadic tribes as well as stationary peoples. Children were taught to weave when they were still small and worked alongside their parents on a single piece. In the early part of the twentieth century, rug weaving was organized into government "factories," which amounted to several weavers making a rug according to a designated pattern in a large room with many other weavers working alongside them on other predesigned rugs. Children were still trained to weave, and one foreman of that period commented that a 5-year-old in his factory would be a good head weaver because by 3 she was selecting colors and by 5 she was directing her own rug. Like a child who plays the piano by ear at the age of 3, it seemed almost as though she had been born with an innate talent.

As a cottage industry, the tradition of Oriental rug weaving has almost passed out of existence. From the example of Soviet sculpture and painting, it is clear "government art" soon loses its freshness and vitality. Unfortunately, many people view the modern Oriental rug industry in this light. It is true that standardized weaving will probably never have the verve and style of the old personal rugs, for two reasons: The designs and colors are not as handsome, and weavers, who have a minimal involvement with these products, often desert the looms for less demanding factory work. The factories use synthetic dyes rather than the natural dyes that gave the older pieces such brilliant coloring and life. Factory-woven rugs may resemble an older rug, but generally speaking they have the insipid quality of an original watered down for economic purposes, like a copy of a Dior. A beige background with black tracery, the motif common to so many factory products, lacks color, warmth, and originality, three traditional and highly sought-after qualities of a good rug. The visual impact is too weak to decorate a room—the rug will only cover the floor.

The logical result of these factors is that good new products are more and more scarce. Weaving is dying out as a family project. Largely through the efforts of the Shahnaz, it is illegal for children to factory weave in Iran. When the Caucasus became a state of the Soviet Union after World War I and many of its tribes were deported to Siberia during World War II, weaving effectively stopped, not to be resumed. It never became a factory industry in that part of the world.

Although this book includes rugs from Turkey, Persia, the Caucasus, India, and China, there are none from Greece, Spain, Bulgaria, Morocco, Poland, Rumania, Japan, Russia, the Mongolian area, and Tibet. In most of these countries thriving industries have developed by copying certain popular types of rugs, like Bokharas, that originally came from other countries. In a way this makes them "fakes," but they are undeniably of Oriental origin. At one time Poland and Rumania made rugs indigenous to themselves, but this is no longer true. In any case, their rugs were never "Oriental" in that their cultural roots were so far from the Middle East. This is not true of Mongolian, Tibetan, and Japanese rugs. Although there are no examples of them here, they are in the Oriental mode but their production is limited and not of the high quality typical of the areas explored here. Each area has some interesting and decorative rugs, but they are few and their rug industries as a whole have never had the standards of the slightly warmer countries. (Although this book begins with Persian rugs, it might be interesting to glance through the Chinese section before beginning because the symbolic representations there are among the oldest in the world.)

So, owing to the penetration of the modern world into the art of a world that traditionally created and nurtured a delicate industry, rug weaving as it was once known is rapidly coming to a close. Today, with so many fine examples of the weaver's craft still in existence and with a more advanced understanding of its context and influences than was possible earlier, we have a unique opportunity to make an assessment that might give future generations some comprehension of the brilliance and variety of Oriental rugs that we accepted as a normal addition to our world. It is all the more important that, as custodians of what are after all original works of art, we do our best to maintain them in the best possible repair and that we give our support and attention to the great collections that exist in the Western world. It is in this spirit that we have written this book.

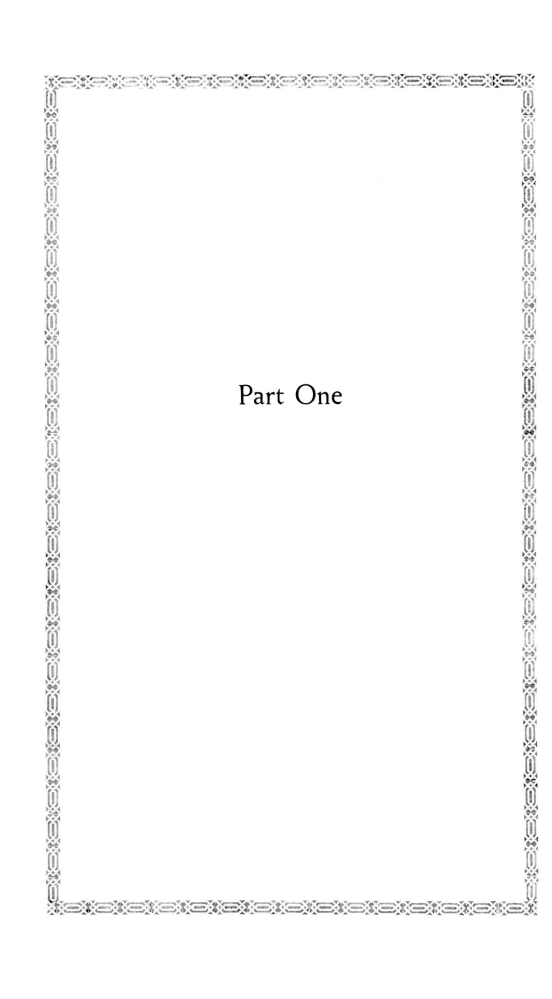

Part One

WEAVING, COLOR, AND AGE

IN THE OLD DAYS the nomads carried little collapsible looms with them in the desert, sometimes weaving for up to eight years on a small rug. The fragments that remain are some of the oldest we have, various and beautiful and, not surprisingly, characterized by charming irregularities on their borders and in the weave that larger rugs woven on stable looms lack. Nowadays almost all Oriental rugs are made in factories, knotted to the rhythms of a chanter who is employed to keep them regular. The weavers are further guided by a pattern and a color card, like a number painting, but in the past they relied on tradition and an experienced eye to guide them. The design of the rug developed as they wove, and whatever they knew came from deep inside to the loom before them.

The big looms are made of four poplar stems and leaned up against a wall, before which the weavers sit on movable stones or stools. The finished part of the rug, which they work lengthwise, is rolled up underneath them as they go. As many as four weavers and a master work on a rug, depending on its size and how soon it is needed. As a rule, a weaver forms 1,400 knots a day, and in Central Persia it takes approximately ten to twelve months to finish a ten-by-thirteen-foot rug.

Oriental rugs are woven on warp threads that run the length of the rug and weft threads that run the width of the rug as well as in and out of the warp. Knots are tied at right angles to the warp and weft and are then sheared to form the pile. (The weft is sometimes known as the woof.) To prepare for weaving, a warp setter climbs to the upper beam of the loom and throws a ball of thread in coordination with a partner on the lower beam until the thread is evenly distributed around both beams. Then the weaver sits in front of the loom and weaves two or three threads of weft, called shoots, in and out of the warp to each row of knots. Balls of colored wool thread hang from the loom, and if the weaver is a traditionalist a knife hangs

Weaving in a factory. Two
weavers, one half-hidden by
the weft threads, sit on an
elevated bench as they work.
Varicolored threads are held
in their laps, and beside them
on a bench are a few diagrams
of the pattern, called *wagirehs*.
The instrument beside the
weaver has teeth on the other
side that are used to tamp
down the knots. Behind is a
similar loom at which a
weaver, again hidden by the
weft threads, may be seen
on the right.

Photograph by Katrina Thomas

from his or her wrist. The rows of weft are pressed down with a comblike instrument.

When the knots are studied, it is almost impossible to see how someone could form 1,400 of them a day. Although we call them knots, they are actually not tied in a knot but threaded delicately at right angles to and through the weft and cut in such a way as to leave the proper length for the pile of the carpet. The Sehna (sometimes spelled Sena) knot is characteristically Persian and is formed in the following manner:

It is used in Central Asia, China and in Persian rugs from Feraghan, Kashan, Khorassan, Meshed, Serabend, Sarouk, Kirman, and Shiraz. Surprisingly, it is not used in the city of Sehna itself.

The other most commonly used knot is the Turkish, or Ghiordes, knot. This knot is used in the Caucasus as well as in Turkey, and often in the Persian towns of Gorevan, Hamadan, Herez, modern Ispahan, Karaja, Kurdistan, Mahal, Muskabad, Niris, Sui-Bulak, and Tabriz. It is formed as follows:

In theory, the Ghiordes knot was invented first. Its collar does render it somewhat thick and inflexible, so the Sehna knot was developed as an alternative. In the Middle East it is called a half-knot, and a good weaver can do either after he or she has gotten into the rhythm.

Although Turkish knots are firmer, the Persian knot may make more delicate designs because the two ends of the thread come out at different places, allowing for more flexibility and refinement of line. In the finished product it is not always easy to tell which knot is used, but generally speaking carpets using the Sehna knot are finer than those using the Ghiordes knot. To check the knotting, fold a rug back on a line of weft. If the yarn covers two warp threads and the ends are together, it is a Turkish knot; if the warp thread is seen between the two ends of the knot, it is Persian. Often the edges of a Persian rug are knotted with the Ghiordes, so it is necessary to look in the body of the rug as opposed to the edge when one checks its knot.

In both cases, the pile of a rug is determined by the direction in which the weaver has finished the knot. This is enhanced by the use of an iron comb, which gives the pile a grain like the direction in which fur grows.

The edges of a rug are finished by techniques that are, as usual, characteristically Persian or Turkish, the Persian overcast and the Turkish selvedged.

Webbing is threaded through the ends of the warp and knotted to keep the rug from fraying. The fringes are as much as four to eight inches from the edge of the carpet, sometimes woven or knotted into a trellis-like pattern for the sake of decoration.

While the rug is being woven, the knotted ends are cropped to a reasonable length with curved shears, but when it is finished the pile is cut by a *perdachtshi*. The *perdachtshi* works by feel, cutting the perfect length with a knife, and his or her skill, entirely dependent on only one sense, may be compared to that of a wine taster or a clock tuner. The Chinese sometimes cut their knots to conform to the pattern, making a bas-relief of the pile and the pattern in the case of modern embossed rugs.

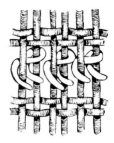

Persian or Sehna knot

Turkish or Ghiordes knot

Overcast

Selvedged

The sides of a rug are finished by overcasting or selvedging. Not surprisingly, each tribe accomplishes this by a characteristic method. A selvedged edge has a thread(s) added for strength, usually in silk or wool. The colors range from brown or dark blue single cords to combinations of pink and brown or red and white, which impart a checked effect.

Knotted fringe

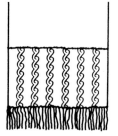

Knotted fringe with
kilim border

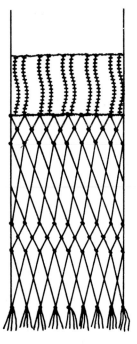

Kilim rug and fringe

Most rugs have a simple
knotted fringe at either end of
the pile, protected by a few
rows of weft. Sometimes
there is a wide band of *kilim*
between the pile and the
fringe, particularly in the
"elephant's foot" rugs from
Central Asia.

Rugs woven entirely in the
kilim style are known for their
extensive knotted fringes,
sometimes as much as two
feet long, which resemble
macramé.

In a linear inch of rug there are from 8 to 60 warp threads and from 2 to 30 knots. In some cases there have been up to 450 knots per square inch of rug, usually in the very old rugs, and now, as a rule, there are 50 to 100.

There are a few important exceptions to these methods of weaving a rug. Bijar rugs, from Kurdistan, are thought of as the thickest and heaviest of Persian rugs. Their knot is an ingenious combination of the Sehna and Ghiordes knots, having the asymmetry of the Sehna but the "collar" of the Ghiordes that gives it its durability.

Some Oriental rugs are not knotted but only woven with warp and weft, which means that one of their distinguishing characteristics is their smooth surface. The best known of these are the Kilims, Soumaks, and Vernés. They are woven in patches of color that, because of the limitations of weaving, are delineated in stepped designs and lack of detail. (In a flat weave it is impossible to outline a curve.) Another interesting facet of the Kilims, for instance, is that they are identical back and front. Sometimes there are open spaces on the vertical lines between colors that are used as part of the design. Other rugs that are not knotted are the Karamans.

Finally, in knotted rugs the fringe is sometimes replaced with a border woven in the Kilim style four to sixteen inches wide, which may be richly embroidered or striped. These highly decorative end borders are called *kilimliks.*

With the exception of nomadic rugs, the warp and weft have almost always been made of cotton and the pile of wool. Sheep's wool is the best, but sometimes camel's hair, silk, goat hair, or angora are used. *Tabachi,* or wool from dead sheep, is removed with lime, but it is not as durable or lustrous as sheared wool. Camel's hair is limited in its use because it is difficult to dye.

As important as the weave of an Oriental rug is its color. An antique Oriental achieves a faded brilliance that is unequaled in any other medium. That these rugs improve with age is a contradiction in terms to a Westerner and makes them all the more fascinating. The best rugs, made with natural dyes, create a wildly original effect because of their lack of uniformity and flawed bite. (The "bite" of a dye, to use the dyer's jargon, is exactly what it sounds like: its ability to grab the fiber to be dyed.) The bite of a natural dye is usually much deeper than that of an artificial dye, but sometimes it hardly bites at all; wool from different sheep does not react uniformly to the properties of natural dyes. The wool is always dyed after it has been spun into thread, so it is never even but, on the contrary, always irregular. The dyes are not fast, and the dyers try to blend the stronger hues with the weak ones. Saffron, for example, renders a pretty but short-lived yellow, so it is blended with pomegranate, whose yellow is less satisfactory but more durable.

At one time, Persian rugs and some Indian rugs were woven in silk colored by vegetable substances mixed into the silkworm's food. These rugs are said to have been of a brilliance and luminosity equaled only in the imagination.

Almost every region has its characteristic colors. Persia is known for crimson and Central Asia for wine red, but probably the most easily recognizable of all is the exotic turkey red of Asia Minor. It is called *dughi* and is made from the madder root by fermentation with curds of sour milk, *kerkerud,* at a time of year when thirty continuous days of sunlight may be depended upon. If it were not for the thirty continuous days, an incomplete fermentation would result. Red is also made from Persian *kermes,* or the dried bodies of insects that live on oak or a species of cactus. In Turkey these insects turn up as the *cochineal,* which are also dried and used in dye. Both are the source of reddish purple, carmine, and violet.

Gul-henna, or henna blossom, is the dye Shiite Muslims use to dye their hair and sometimes their animals on festive occasions to honor Allah. They also use it to dye their hair as they age. In the West, "hennaed hair" is an occasional fashion fad. The color, a warm reddish-brown, is often seen in Oriental rugs, and even the henna plant is sometimes represented in the Sultanabad motif or Herati design.

Still another red may be made from cherries.

Brown, *catechu* or *cutch,* is made from gall apples, or nut galls, and the darkest brown is made from oak apples. Yellow is made from pomegranate rind, saffron, and turmeric. Buckthorn berries are used in the Caucasus, Anatolia, and Kurdistan for a striking orange-yellow that is unique but is too hard a color for large surfaces. Green is made by mixing indigo with one of the yellow dyes.

Black is sometimes just the wool of a very dark sheep, but more often it is a mordant made from gallic acid (a mordant is a substance that, when mixed with a dyestuff, creates a fixed color for a fiber). Another way to make black is to mix logwood with an iron salt like ferrous sulphate, which again acts as a mordant. The black dyes have a corrosive effect on wool, causing the first deterioration in a rug's pile. Semi-antique rugs with incomplete black outlines are often seen.

The most fabulous dye in the world is the blue made from the indigo plant. It is so versatile that the Persians have three words for it in their vocabulary: *nil* for indigo, *surmey* for the deepest color, and *abi* for the lightest. Indigo is combined with hydrosulphate in a wood vat. The wool is dipped, and when it is reexposed to light it turns blue. It is never unmixed, so in a sense there is no true indigo.

The water and sunlight are so unpredictable that some of the best colors are made by chance. Streaks, or *abrash,* are not regarded as flaws by Easterners but are considered part of the charm of the whole rug. They do not see perfection as regularity, an idea that seems primitive at first but on reflection may be very sophisticated.

Nowadays synthetic dyes are probably as good as natural dyes, but not as attractively irregular, and the sheen or polish of an old rug may be simulated. A machine-made rug, which can be easily detected by looking at the back, has a restricted color range as well as limitations in duplicating the detail of an old design.

The knowledge that has come to us of early rugs is as romantic as indigo blue. In 1949 a rug was found by the Russian archaeologist Rudenko six miles from the border of Outer Mongolia. It had been preserved in a sheet of ice since the Scythian Period in the fifth century B.C.

The rug itself, known as the Pasyrik Rug, has the cryptic quality of a checkerboard, which its field resembles. Within each square is a St. Andrew's cross. Bordering this are five bands, each designed in a regular pattern of horses, griffins, men, more St. Andrew's crosses, and elks. The widest border, a pattern of horsemen, is similar to a bas-relief seen at Persepolis and is also found in Assyrian art. The outside band is marked with two heavy black indicators, a fact that has given rise to

Sehna

Ghiordes

Persian or Sehna knot. In these diagrams, the white, wormlike shapes indicate knots. Unfortunately, it is difficult to visualize knots from drawings because of the lack of perspective. Although the knots appear to lie flat, their ends actually stand up to create the pile directly over the warp threads rather than parallel to them. The knot and its ends are as perpendicular to the warp threads as the weaver can make them.

There are two other aspects to keep in mind when perusing this type of diagram: (1) A rug is made up of thousands of knots like this, all packed in together as tightly as possible. Above and below this row are hundreds like it. (2) The knot may go around more than two warp threads. Often it goes around four. When it goes around eight, it is called a *jufti* knot; the weave is considered to be too loose by connoisseurs, and the buyer is thought to be cheated.

speculation that the rug was meant to be used as the basis of a game, possibly something like Parcheesi or checkers. The Pasyrik carpet was woven in the Ghiordes knot at 270 knots per square inch.

The Pasyrik carpet poses far more questions than it solves. All it really tells us is that pile carpet weaving existed in its present form long before it was generally thought to have developed. Pasyrik is a hamlet in the Altai mountain range where the Scyths, a nomadic tribe whose beginnings are thought to have been in Persia, had wandered. Like the Egyptians, their nobles constructed elaborate underground tombs in which to bury their belongings. These included superbly crafted gold jewelry, all manner of household and transportation effects, and another rug. This is called the Bachadan rug after its excavation site and is knotted in the Sehna knot at 450 knots per square inch, but is far less distinctive than the Pasyrik. Fragments of pile cloths, felt, Kilims, and tapestry were also found at the Scythian sites and may be seen at the Hermitage Museum in Leningrad.

The next-oldest rug fragments were found at Noin-Ula in the Turfan district of Eastern Turkestan. They were judged to have been made between the third and sixth centuries A.D. Excavated by Sir Aurel Stein, Le Coq, and the German expeditions, they were destroyed with the Berlin Museum during World War II.

Aside from their age, two aspects of this cache are worthy of note. First, their design included some of the classic motifs still seen today, such as the Sejshour's running-dog border from the Caucasus. Second, Turfan is on the old trade route that brought silk from China across Asia, establishing the possibility that such a route existed centuries even before the birth of Christ.

Al Fostat, another archaeological site that has yielded rug fragments, lies outside of Cairo. Once the capital of Egypt, it was decimated during the twelfth century. So far over 100 fragments have been found, dating from the ninth century A.D. (estimated) to the thirteenth, fourteenth, and fifteenth centuries, the period that produced most of these rugs. Oddly enough, the origins of the rugs in this group are not immediately recognizable, but they have been ascribed to Persia, the Caucasus, and Asia Minor. A few of these many fragments show a progression from flat to pile weaving. For example, in Deir-el-Bahri a looped textile was found dating from before 2160 B.C. Simply woven, the loops were no more than weft threads drawn loosely out over certain warp threads that passed firmly through others. The loops were not sheared or cut, so the surface, while not flat, was not tufted either. Probably at some point the weavers did begin to either cut or shear the loops. In any case, in the fourteenth century B.C. they had begun to wrap a continuous weft thread around the warp in such a way that it could be pulled up to cut, which of course produced a pile. The technique itself is somewhat ungainly but is still very close to the individual Sehna and Ghiordes knots. Oddly enough, the Egyptian method of wrapping the weft threads around the warp produced a knot structure similar to both but identical to neither. It had a collar like the Ghiordes knot yet was asymmetrical like the Sehna knot.

Early examples of nomadic weaving were found in the Alaeddin mosque in Konya in the Turkish interior, and date from near the end of the fourteenth century. Called

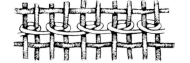

Soumak weave

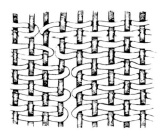

Kilim weave

Soumak technique. The thread may be wrapped around one warp thread, or there may be two rows of Soumak weaving between the weft threads. Kilim technique. The continuous thread is broken when a different color is needed, as, for example, on the left and the right sides of this diagram. As illustrated, this creates an unattached space between colors and explains why this technique is somewhat known as "slit weave."

the Seljuk carpets, although very poorly conserved, they are now in the Evtaf Museum in Istanbul. They are woven in small geometric patterns of white, black, blue, and red.

The very old rugs are fairly easy to identify because there are so few of them that they are all known and they are too finely made and delicately woven to make the cost of duplication feasible. The classic period for Persia is the sixteenth century, for Turkey the seventeenth. Interestingly, some of the Turkish rugs dating from the sixteenth century are woven in the Sehna knot.

During the Safavid dynasty, from 1502 to 1736, the Muslim dictum against representation of living creatures in art was relaxed, resulting in "garden carpets," filled with flowers and animals on what was often a trellis-like design, and "hunting rugs" depicting armed men on foot or horseback following their prey, the wild beasts, in a stylized forest. A sixteenth-century Persian rug was usually woven with about 230 Sehna knots per square inch, three shoots of silk weft, some metal threads, simple finishing on the sides, a two-level warp, and a warp fringe. They used only about ten colors, although by that time vegetable dyes had been found and refined for a fuller range of color. In the seventeenth century the warp had changed from wool to cotton, which is stronger and less liable to stretch, and the texture of the rug was not as fine, having decreased to 175 knots per square inch. No metal thread was used. The weavers still limited themselves to ten colors in a rug, but in the space of a century the palette had changed.

Characteristic of the classic periods is superlative design. The all-over patterns have rhythm and balance, which today invariably degenerate into ostentation, imitation, and lack of proportion. The arabesque, for example, which is so graceful in the classic period, today becomes heavy, thick, and unwieldy, more like snakes than vines.

In the late sixteenth and early seventeenth centuries a group of rugs were woven in Herat, India, by Persians who may have been imported to work for Akbar. The combination of the hot Indian colors and the intricate Persian designs imparts a rare quality of sensuality and luxury to these rugs. They were woven with 175 Sehna knots per square inch on a two-level silk or cotton warp with three shoots of cotton weft. The pile was wool, with occasional patches of white cotton.

The earliest Ushak rugs from Asia Minor date from the fifteenth to the seventeenth centuries. They are made on a one-level warp of white wool with a two-shoot weft of red wool and knotted in a coarse Ghiordes. The pile is wool and, in the early ones, sometimes cotton. Until the end of the sixteenth century they were made with 70 knots per square inch in seven colors, later increasing to 85 knots. "Transylvania" rugs, also from Asia Minor, have a warp and weft of dyed yellow, up to 70 knots per square inch, and as many as nine colors.

A few rugs have been dated and signed by their makers. Around 1700, when weaving was a high art under the patronage of the court, it became the fashion in Persia and Turkey for the weaver to sign a rug, but after the golden era few weavers identified themselves.

At the beginning of the twentieth century it once again became popular to claim one's work, and a few master weavers like Serafian signed their names. An example of this style may be seen in the Ispahan (Plate 7), where a signature has been marked into the *kilim* at the bottom of the rug. As a rule, before Serafian the signature and the date (if there was one) were woven into a corner of the rug itself. In their time and later these signatures were emulated, with the result that many rugs have been falsely attributed to these masters. Some of these "old" new rugs are dated around the start of World War I, and they are the last dated rugs. But even without this complication a dated rug is difficult to verify. Most dates are worked in Arabic numbers according to the Muhammadan chronology (to change to our system, subtract 1/33 of their number and add 622). The Arabic numbers are read backwards, and their mark for 1000, a raised dot, · , is omitted in a date. The two (٢) and the three (٣) may easily be changed to simulate each other, and many dates have been forged since the end of the nineteenth century.

Aniline, the first chemical dye used in the East, was introduced in the 1860s, and by the 1870s other chemical dyes were being used as well. If the color of a rug is tested and found to be other than vegetable, it is dated after the time when its particular dye type was introduced.

Generally speaking, there are several other signs of age to be aware of. White changes to cream, and black wool, as mentioned earlier, breaks down first. The back of a new rug is fuzzy and that of an old one smooth; the front of a new rug is harsh, that of an old one smooth; and of course the design and look of a new rug are rough and a bit harsh while an old one might have more elegance and character.

The new factory-made rugs are often put on the market as antiques. They copy the old designs and are chemically treated to simulate the look of an antique, but one thing that almost always gives them away as new rugs is their "wonderful condition." Being new rugs, they *should* be in wonderful condition, albeit stiff and unworn. By contrast, the rugs that are as supple as velvet and have not been worn although old or antique, are the ones that command the highest prices in today's market.

0	1	2	3	4	5	6	7	8	9

Arabic numerals

BUYING AND SELLING

G. GRIFFIN LEWIS, the foremost rug expert of his day, wrote as follows: "The author wishes especially to call attention to the great change in the prices of rugs. . . . Good antique pieces have advanced from 300% to 800% and commercial pieces from 100% to 400%." Mr. Lewis wrote this in 1920, but it could have been written yesterday. He complained that "with carpets, much unnecessary floor space must be covered, which represents so much waste money."[1] He estimated, in tones of amazement, that good rugs cost from sixty cents to ten dollars a square foot.

As an investment, the value of antique and old Oriental rugs has gone steadily upward, at least since the beginning of this century. Until now, the highest rug prices in modern history were paid in the 1920s, but over the past fifteen years they have increased as much as tenfold. The results of a survey published in July 1973 by an English magazine, *The Antiques Finder,* showed eighteen rugs, chosen at random from nineteenth-century production, to have increased in value between 1951 and 1973 by an average ratio of sixteen to one. In 1978, rugs are safer than the stock market. Their appeal to investors is evidenced by the frequency with which they appear in the sales catalogs of auction galleries and by the multiplying number of dealers. In 1973 alone the market experienced what the *Wall Street Journal* referred to as a "dramatic rise" in prices, which in some instances amounted to as much as 100 percent. The *Journal* attributed this surge to the higher price of wool and to then-current dollar devaluations. Aside from these considerations is this rather curious reflection of taste: The European demand for Oriental rugs has always been greater than the American demand, to the extent that an Oriental rug is almost a house uniform to certain classes, and a tremendous quantity of rugs is absorbed in the European market, forcing prices up everywhere else. Last but not least is the perennial bogey of Westernization, currently taking place in Iran and Turkey. Labor is more expensive than ever before; many former weavers prefer to work in a new factory; and rugs are no longer these nations' biggest industry.

The rise in prices, while substantial, has not been uniform. For example, certain Chinese rugs have risen four times in price, some three. Again, while a few Anatolian types have risen ten times in price, others have risen only twofold. The price rises have not been exact—just spectacular. Of course, one of the main factors is fashion, and in the past nine years the Kazaks, Caucasian Dragons, Ladik prayer rugs, and Turkoman Tekkes, among others, have undergone the greatest price increases. Conversely, the value of a group of rugs decreases when the market is deluged with Indian or Pakistani copies, as in the case of Bokharas.

Not surprisingly, an investment in an antique is more quickly realizable than in a new rug. At the outset, however, antiques are decidedly more expensive, as witness the nineteenth-century rugs noted in *The Antiques Finder*. (An antique, to the trade, is a rug that is 100 years old or more, a semi-antique one that is 50 to 100 years old.)

A rug collector values rarity. The person who wants to buy a rug that may be used at home but that is also an investment considers the number of knots per square inch, the quality and depth of the colors, and beauty of design. Of a more practical nature is the condition of the rug. It should be clean, whole, not unevenly worn, not discolored, and not extensively repaired or rewoven (work done on the edges and warp is natural).

A rug that does not lie flat on the floor can today be corrected by a process of "stretching." Otherwise, the places that stick up, aside from being dangerous, wear out first.

Photograph © 1972 by George Holton

Bazaar in Teheran.

It is not uncommon for the underweave of a rug to disintegrate before the pile, from mildew or because it is not wool. To check its strength, turn the rug back and fold it against the warp and then against the weft. Should it split or crack, before long it will be too dilapidated to use.

Another important factor is that the wool be in good condition, elastic and springy. Inspect for the wool's quality to guard against "dead" wool. When the rug is on the floor, look at how the light plays on the pile, and turn the rug so you can see how it appears from several angles. If the pile is thin, the rug will only need more care.

The "aging" process of a new rug can be very damaging. Because the colors of a new vegetable-dyed rug are too harsh to be pleasing to a Westerner, or in an effort to simulate an antique, both the weavers and the importers have subjected many rugs to various washes to soften their colors. These range from lime juice or boracic acid to chemicals. Some of the new washes are not destructive, but if an old rug has been subjected to, say, chlorine, the pile will be noticeably fuzzy and unhealthy looking. (By contrast, another wash can produce the sheen that normally appears only after years of use.) Sometimes the "aging" process includes burying the rugs for months after they have been woven. Several years ago a friend of ours drove a rented car through the bazaar, where he had strayed by mistake, at Shiraz. Hearing the car, a family ran out and threw a new rug in his path. He stopped to back up, but they enthusiastically waved him over the rug. After he had driven over it they concluded that the rug was much improved, and a little distance further he similarly accommodated another family. They explained that it "tightened the weave" and aged the rug.

Another spurious practice is painting, in which color is applied superficially to a carpet to camouflage worn spots. This is fairly easy to detect by a close visual inspection of the pile or by what is casually known as the handkerchief test. This consists of an application of same, damp with spit, to the suspected areas of the rug. If it has in fact been painted, the handkerchief will come away colored.

Aside from the condition of the rug, one must buy from the right place and pay the right price. A definite market value exists for every rug at every time, and the optimum price is that value or less. A good way of acquainting oneself with current prices, aside from canvassing the area (starting with the big department stores and going on to the serious dealers) is to purchase the catalogs of the good auction houses. Lefevre in London, Sotheby's and Christie's in London and New York and the Plaza Art Galleries in New York have all had fascinating rug sales in the past few years.

Of course, there is no substitute for a reputable dealer, in terms of practical knowledge of the market, sources, and information. Ideally, the dealer will be the kind of person who parts with a rug he or she has owned for years and loves greatly rather than telling you about the wonderful pieces that are *not* for sale. The dealer will back a purchase with a guarantee, resell a rug, and let customers try out their choices at home. In the rug business, a dealer with a "no return" policy might be hawking suspect goods. The dealer should point out uneven wear, cuts, missing details of the border and ends, and hidden reductions in size.

Auctions are the Circe of the world of art and artifacts. They take advantage of one's greed and the belief that one might get something for nothing or find the treasure everyone else has missed. At the very least, they give one an opportunity to re-affirm what one has always known, that one is a superior gambler, or a gambler in control. An auction is a drama where one may be an actor or a spectator. The sound of the gavel is very exhilarating, and hardly anything is so much fun. Auction wares are almost always exhibited in advance, and the temptation is to just give them a fast look before bidding. Because they are notoriously refurbished, painted, dirtied up, dyed, or not shown under a true light, this convenient method of shopping is most unwise. Unfortunately, the auctioneer counts on the customer's cursory appraisal of the merchandise to make sales.

Many auction rugs come from dealers who regularly auction pieces they would not be willing to back with their own name. In any case, all the items are "reserved" at prices that are profit making for the dealer, plus the auctioneer's commission. It is easy to end up paying prices that are higher than retail for bad merchandise. Although the public is generally aware that auction goods are bought on an "as is" basis, when applied to rugs this means no guarantee of age, no indication of hidden defects, and most important, no chance of anticipating how the rug will look in your house.

Another aspect of auctions is that they are almost always a dealer's market, like furniture and art auctions. Dealers, whose markup may be 100 percent, dominate the bidding, and they know what they are doing. If you see an auction rug you must have, you should ask an expert's opinion, set a maximum price, and stick to it.

Having read this far, it is no doubt clear that on the right day one might get more for an old rug in an auction than from a dealer. This is true, taking into account the auctioneer's fee. Selling at auction can be particularly lucrative if one has several rugs and time to wait for the money. In this case a preliminary decision should be made: whether to sell all the rugs or to be left with those that do not reach reserve prices. And often many do not. A dealer will of course give you cash for the lot.

One final aspect of buying and selling should be stressed: The decorative qualities of an Oriental rug are as elusive as a Calder mobile out of their element. A rug hung for display will look totally different on your floor, and a photogenic rug may not be as appealing before your eyes, so a bit of experimentation is often required to select the right rug.

LIVING WITH AN ORIENTAL RUG

SOME OF THE BEST things in life wear out. Most people would prefer to forget this fact, particularly when buying a rug so fine it is an investment, but it is impossible to forget when one realizes that the price of an old rug depends on its condition. The reason there are so few good rugs left of the ones that came to Europe and the United States at the beginning of this century is that they were not costly and therefore were treated carelessly. Fine Shirvans are abused as entrance mats in farmhouses, and highly perishable silk rugs are placed under diningroom tables. It is true that an Oriental rug can take an astonishing amount of wear—usually five to ten times what wall-to-wall carpeting can take—and, if well looked after, will last a lifetime. However, *gutta cavat lapidem*—a drop of water will wear away a stone. Caring for a rug is a constant job, but not a difficult one. One need not take one's shoes off to walk on it as they do in the East, but it is important to keep it clean and dry. More will be said on this subject after a few points of common sense.

Since a rug takes the hardest wear on the floor, it should be laid carefully over a rubber or felt mat (or both) and rotated in place every six months to distribute the wear as evenly as possible. A rug placed before the front door naturally has more dirt tracked onto it than one on a less-used floor, and a sturdy rug should be selected for use under a diningroom table, where the center of the rug is protected but the contours are subject to uneven wear. Heavy pieces of furniture with concentrated points of weight, like the legs of a standing chest, tend to break down the pile. When this is unavoidable, casters may act as a cushion, although they are a distraction in aesthetic terms. Hanging a small rug may be decorative, but it is advisable only if you know the weft or warp threads are strong enough to support it, as hanging exerts a pressure on them that they were not designed to bear.

An example of the blend of old world and new so often seen in the Middle East. This weaver is cleaning his new rug, woven painstakingly by hand, with *Tide*. Although the rug is probably clean, new rugs are always washed before they are put on the market to remove the excess vegetable dye.

Photograph by Carl Purcell

For storage, a rug should be rolled, not folded, as the weft and warp tend to wear out along the fold lines. If rugs are to be stored in the home, they should be rolled up with a moth deterrent, wrapped in heavy paper, and placed in a dry room. Moths can actually be a problem whether a rug is in or out of storage, winter or summer, so it is advisable to have your rugs professionally mothproofed at least once a year. Your rugs may also be placed in commercial cold storage, a service most good rug cleaners provide.

Mildew, the curse of a damp climate, has destroyed many wool rugs. If you notice it, a reputable dealer will advise you on how to get rid of it. If a rough breaking sound is heard when the rug is bent back, the chances are that mildew has already rotted the weft.

Like the finest silk scarf, an Oriental rug eventually needs to be cleaned in soap and water, a process that debilitates the fiber. Consequently, your rug-preservation strategy should be to keep the rug clean with a minimum of washing. The best method of everyday cleaning is vacuuming with the grain of the pile. The fringe, which holds the rug together, is more fragile than the pile and should not be vacuumed. As with everything else in life, there are fashions in rug cleaning, and at this writing beating is out. Pay no heed to the ladies in the bazaar and on Mediterranean balconies—it seems that they have been wrong for centuries and that beating is too hard on the rug's foundation. Nor should rugs be shaken violently. Beating is countenanced only when the rug is lying face down in the snow—which is, incidentally, the most esoteric method of rug cleaning and dates from time immemorial.

A good method of washing a rug at home is to use an oil-based soap followed by a rinse of vinegar or lemon and water (the ratio is sixteen parts of water to one part of acid) to take out the soap. One may also use one of the commercial foam cleaners that is vacuumed off after it dries, but it should be left on a few hours longer than directed because if the rug is vacuumed before it is completely dry the dirt may be ground further into the wool threads. For the same reason (and to avoid mildew), try to keep the rug as dry as possible at home.

Unless it is laid in a very active part of the house, a rug need not be cleaned professionally more than once every couple of years, and in some cases only every four or five years. Many "professionals" merely use a chemical solution not too different from the ones on the market, but a soap-and-water wash is best. Some cleaning plants use rotary brushes on the surface of the rug and immerse it for rinsing, but a machine with a wringer and a jet spray is equally good, because the rug dries as quickly as possible.

Part Two

PERSIA

PERSIAN RUGS have gained a reputation as the finest in the world. They are the basis of many collections, and are included in almost all. It is nearly axiomatic that the student of Oriental rugs, after an initial infatuation with the vibrance of the Caucasians, loses his or her heart for life to the deep, serene complexity of the Persians.

The area called Persia is almost as large and just as diverse as the United States. It is west of India, east of Asia Minor, south of Russia, and separated from Saudi Arabia only by the narrow sliver of the Persian Gulf, which at one time must not have existed at all. Because of its early success as a political unit of international consequence, Persia has for centuries been at the very center of Middle Eastern life, both intellectually and geographically. Now the value of oil is putting modern Iran in a position of renewed power.

Over a period longer by twenty-two centuries than the history of the United States, an equal number of peoples of diverse ethnic and social types have settled in Persia and lived together, and each has left an undeniable imprint. It is a land of startling contrasts, from huge areas of desert to cosmopolitan cities such as Teheran. The life styles emerging from these conditions have been those of the tribal nomad and the settled metropolitan toiler. Not surprisingly, Persian rugs are as varied as their origins, having a multitude of patterns, sizes, and color preferences. What is surprising is the overall fineness and level of quality emerging from a past that historians represent as barbaric and from a present in which progress is equated with more machinery and less hand work. Persia is the only place in the world where one can—or ever could—purchase a new rug woven with more than 800 knots per square inch.

Persia has one of the oldest traditions of pile knotting in the world. Although the time of its inception is unclear, there are reasons to assume that it was fairly early. Geographically, Persia lies in the heart of the rug-weaving world, and much of the land is subject to extremely cold winters. Sheep are indigenous to Persia, and it is known that flat-woven products were developed very early by the nomadic tribes. Although Herodotus mentioned rugs as early as the fifth century B.C. and the jeweled rug of Khusrau was reported in the sixth century A.D., there is a possibility that these coverings were tapestry or felt. Both of these techniques are known to have been developed in Persia and China earlier than pile weaving. (Tapestry is a process in which work in threads is laid over a basic weaving structure, just as pile knotting is, but in a tapestry the knots are smoothly finished. Felt is made from matted fibers worked into cloth, not by weaving but by applying a rolling pressure together with a liquid.) It is certain, however, that the ninth-century Arab geographer Hadudal'-Alam referred to pile carpets when he wrote that they were woven in Fars, the southern district on the Persian Gulf. In the tenth century the geographers Istahri and Mukaddasi commented on rugs in the Qainat and on certain prayer rugs they had seen. The period from the fifteenth through the seventeenth centuries was the high-water mark of Persian rug weaving, and the style that emerged during that period is still dominant today. For that complexity of design, that mastery of dye, that expertise in translating the pattern to a tufted weave, and that delicacy of the knot itself to have been achieved by the fifteenth century, there must already have been centuries of development.

Persia is the largest homogeneous rug-weaving area in the East, that is, the largest social and political unit. More rugs have come from its looms for export than from any other region. As a result, one's stereotype of an Oriental rug is often Persian. Since at one time almost all Oriental wares passed through Istanbul in transit to the Western market, many rugs were labeled "Turkey" that were probably Persian. Among the rich colonials in America, for instance, it is not uncommon to see orders for a "Turkey rug, 14 by 18 feet," and so forth as early as the seventeenth century. The rug delivered, while labeled "Turkey," could have been Persian. This error was common in other fields of trade, such as ceramics, bronzes, and upholstery cloth.

It could be said that for hundreds of years the grand tradition of the Persian rug has been one of homage to the garden, the style brought to its highest point under the patronage of Shah Abbas in the late sixteenth and early seventeenth centuries. This shah was the first to establish ateliers for weavers and artists, the forerunners of modern rug factories. Attesting to the brilliant results of his patronage is the fact that the characteristic designs of his period are still being elaborated on in "new" models such as the species called the meditation rug (the rather unfortunate trade name of a more than respectable twentieth-century rug, discussed at further length with Plate 4). The focus of the Shah Abbas classic is usually a medallion on a floral background organized by an arabesque and surrounded by four or more borders. As Arthur Upham Pope, a historian to whom all students of the Middle East are in debt, has pointed out, the carpet is composed of several highly structured designs that occasionally meet, like the melodic lines of a symphony, combining to create a harmony. A Feraghan rug (Plate 4), the Victorian Englishman's "Ford" rug, has at least five layers of design. Many of the modern abstract artists, like Willem de Kooning or Jackson Pollock, construct their works by using several layers of design at the same time that are not primarily illustrative of depth but add to the cumulative surface decoration. Fresh details come to light in both a de Kooning and a good Persian rug even after one thinks one has lived with it long enough to know it well.

It is possible that these large, formal, complex carpets would have been produced only by a group effort, as conceived by Shah Abbas or by a Western buyer a few centuries later. Their production involves many people—shepherds, dyers, spinners, artists, weavers, and businessmen. Alongside this tradition is the tribal rug, in which one person plays all of these parts. The tribal and factory rugs themselves are as much in antithesis as their method of production. Tribal rugs are small, the designs straight-lined, the colors few, the knotting loose, the looms movable. The curves of a large floral rug, on the other hand, are plotted on a scale paper called a *wagireh*. In rough parlance, this diagram of knots and colors performs the function of a cartoon for a Renaissance painting or tapestry. The tribal weavers, whose work is more casual, use many of the same pictorial ideas but weave them in straight lines, eliminating the need for the *wagireh*, the artist, and the fineness of knotting. The result, like a Heriz rug (Plate 6), is striking, and while it is quite different from, for example, an Ispahan, it is based on the same pictorial elements. The other recurrent tribal design is three medallions down the center, like the Kurdistan in Plate 11.

Various tribes have played an active part in Persian history. They are the Kurds, Lurs, Bakhtiari, Kashgai, Khamseh, Shahsevans, Arabs, and Baluchi. The Lurs, makers of the Luristan pottery seen in every museum in the world, produce rugs only recently revalued, but most of the rest produce carpets that are not only striking but which constitute today's collectors' items. Their rugs, while bright and coarse, have a virility notably lacking in more refined products.

In several instances certain tribes have achieved a dissident strength of such force as to warrant transplantation, and for this reason one occasionally finds a rug from the south of Persia that has decidedly northern characteristics, like the Afshahari in Plate 20. In the twentieth century the Pahlavi shahs, in an effort to achieve internal stability, have resettled the native tribes several times.

The sheer force of design and volume of output demonstrated by the Persians forces one to ask why. The answer lies in numerous factors: Persia's geographic mix, location, history, and religion have combined to create a climate in which such unusual artistic growth could take place.

For centuries the natural topography of Persia would support little more than no-madic peoples. Two sides of the land are enclosed by high mountains: the Elborz Range, which crosses north from Turkey to the Caucasus, and the Zagros Range, which goes down the western boundary of Iraq to the Persian Gulf. Mt. Ararat, where Noah's ark is said to have come to rest after the flood subsided, is on the Turkish side of the Elborz. The oil fields are mainly in the south of Iran, near Kuwait and Saudi Arabia. The land lying between the cleft of the mountain ranges is tanta-mount to a plateau 4000 feet above sea level, saline and dry. The population centers are on the steppes and foothills of the mountain ranges, where it is cooler, except for a line of cities extending from Teheran to Agra, India, that includes Qum, Kashan, Joshagan, Ispahan, Yezd, and Kirman. The great desert, called "the Lut," is east of Persia, stretching north hundreds of miles to the Elborz Range.

Between Firdaus and Yezd there are 408 miles of unsettled desert. Firdaus itself is an ancient oasis, complete with palm trees and battlements. In Firdaus, as well as most other towns, many citizens dwell in mud houses that are actually a line of rooms with a common wall between them and a continuous roof that in an aerial view looks like a strip of adjoining half-bubbles. Here the poverty of the desert produced the first apartment houses. The plateau is so dry that its rivers never reach the sea. In these regions the nomads moved with the seasons to pastures green enough to support life, weaving their rugs on portable looms.

By contrast, Teheran is a large, modern city rather like Johannesburg, and in the northwest corner of the country, west of the Caspian Sea, is a wet, green farming region.

Persian civilization has been recorded since the sixth century B.C., and like China, its artistic traditions have evolved over centuries. Unlike China, the different groups of conquerors that have swept over Persia have markedly changed its artistic style, as have the different religious influences. Whereas in China the Buddhist and Confucian symbols are drawn by the same hand, in Persia the Muslim decoration is markedly different from the style of the Achaemenians, for example.

As a vast plateau at the crossroads of a large geographic region, Persia has been subject to the influence of numerous races and the vagaries of many foreign potentates. It has been a pawn to the colonial greed of other nations, but the Persian personality has survived, if not dominated, its conquerors. As a result, Persia's history has been one of change, of possession and slavery, and of disorganization. Persian history has the capricious quality of a desert windstorm. For centuries the land was dominated by assimilated foreigners who protected themselves by means of a feudal system. It is evident from a short recounting of Persia's political history that what is now known as "Islamic art" has come together over a long period from a variety of influences—Persian, Indian, Greek, Mongolian, Chinese, Turkish, and Arabian, to name the most dominant. By the time rug weaving is known to have begun in Persia, the weavers had a long heritage of influences from conquerors and conquered alike.

Persia was first populated by members of the Aryan tribe who spread to the region below the Caspian Sea. They called this region Iran. Their language was Persian, or Fars, and was written in Arabic. The Greeks called the land Parsa in the time of the Achaemenians. The southern province on the Persian Gulf is today called Fars.

In an international context, the only time Iran has been as powerful as it is now was in the sixth century B.C. When Cyrus the Great overthrew his Median king in 553 B.C. he laid the foundation for an empire that was to include Armenia, Asia Minor, Parthia, Bactria, Chorasnia on the Greek coast of the Mediterranean, Babylon, and Egypt. The Achaemenians numbered Xerxes and Darius among their rulers. They introduced the first period of great Persian art. In addition to enormous halls at Susa and Ecbatana, they built Persepolis, the Versailles of the Achaemenians. These massive stone palaces were sustained by avenues of arches and decorated with bas-relief carvings of one-dimensional figures.

The walls were also ornamented with multicolored tiles, which had an obvious resemblance to later Persian rug designs, and the whole already showed a predilection for flat surface decoration rather than perspective drawings. Records exist indicating that textiles and metalwork were produced at this time, five centuries before the birth of Christ.

The Achaemenian rule was overthrown by Alexander the Great, who defeated Darius the Third in 336 and burned Persepolis. He was followed by the Parthian Greeks and the Sassanians, who were Zoroastrians. After they conquered Byzantium they brought Roman and Byzantine influences to Persia. The Parthian overlord was known as the "king of kings," or shahinshah, and the Parthians wrote in an Arabic script called *pahlavi*, the name later chosen by the present dynasty.

In the Sassanian era the arch, vault, and dome were developed. Regardless of how they began, the typical Sassanian arch eventually became pointed, like the Buddhist arch in India. The typical Persian dome eventually bulged against the sky under a squat, pointed arch. It was gold or blue decorated with black and white *kufic* letters or arabesques, all in tile. The effect of these domes against the sky is typically one of a decorated flat surface rather than one of dimensions, scale, and perspective. The perspective of the dome against the sky is irrelevant. It is also interesting to note that the line of a dome is identical to the curve of a medallion or the reverse of an arabesque. The medallions one now sees on the rugs are actually very like the ones on the earliest pottery from the Sassanian period. Their striking artistic influence was one of dignity but also of rhythm and simplicity.

Historically, the outstanding artistic eras have corresponded to periods of spiritual rebirth or depth, and certainly the advent of the Islamic religion in Persia had that effect. Abu Bekr, the first caliph and the successor of Muhammed, conquered the Sassanians in 641. During this period Arab geographers and historians kept fuller records than before and for the first time referred to pile carpets as we know them. But the Islamic influence that swept through Persia dominated all aspects of life, from faith to carpets. This was true not only of Persia but also of other antique cultures thought to be indigenous, like that of India. Literally and symbolically, the mosque kept vigil from the Samarkand to Gibraltar. Baghdad was the center of this empire, with important capitals in Samarkand, Damascus, Cairo, and Ray. It was a culture that mixed many groups—Indians, Turks, Copts, Persians, and Byzantine Greeks. In art, the Muslim dictum against the representation of living animals and people contributed to the continuing development of floral or geometric surface design.

In 1055 the Seljuks overcame Baghdad, and their sultans ruled Persia from 1037 to 1194. As an army of would-be conquerors the Turks were barbaric and cruel in their campaigns across Persia, but as victors their reign was beneficial and surprisingly constructive. Their empire included the Caucasus as well as Asia Minor and Mesopotamia. Although the Turks ruled, they were assimilated by the Persians, as the Sassanians had been before them. They became Muslims and patronized the Persian arts: painting, architecture, and calligraphy. At that time Arabic was used, and it gained popularity because it is quite a lot simpler than *pahlavi*. Although there are numerous references to rugs from this period, rug weaving was regarded as no more than a household craft and consequently did not benefit from the patronage of the ruling class.

The Mongols ruled for three centuries after the Turks. Although Genghis Khan, Hulagu Khan, and Tamerlane are best known for their destructive military rampages, in times of peace their patronage produced interesting artistic periods, largely as a result of the increased Chinese trade. The Mongols imported Chinese porcelain artists, who brought with them the phoenix, lotus, key, cartouche, and fretwork, and whose square seals evolved into the *kufic* writing style. What is even more important is that the Persians' contact with the Chinese accelerated their own work in textiles, and Persia began to produce silk, velvet, and brocade.

In one area they far surpassed anything that had been done before. The decorated book, often with a medallion embossed on the leather cover, was cultivated as an art form, and the miniatures from those fourteenth- and fifteenth-century books are remarkable for their wealth of detail executed in minute terms. They include every facet and artifact of courtly life, some of which are surprisingly Chinese, like a trellised bridge over a garden brook. They are interesting not only because they show ornamental rugs or tapestries but also because they are the aesthetic forerunners of the rugs of the Great Safavian Epoch. At times the entire surface would be covered with a multitude of small one-dimensional figures in a scene that would include brocades, plants and flowers of all sorts, animals, and books. Usually the size of the figures was as out of line as the perspective, and there would be a splendid leafy figure, for example, that dwarfed a man, rather like a Rousseau painting. Of course, the effect of such a design is ultimately abstract.

Some of the miniatures show rather advanced rugs. The Venetian ambassador to the court of Uzun Hassan of the White Sheep Dynasty in the fifteenth century mentioned carpets, a few of which are known to have come from Fars. The Mongols' work in mosaics was also exemplary. Under the Safavid shahs each of these elements would be used to even greater effect in carpet weaving.

In the sixteenth century Ismail founded the Safavid Dynasty. He was the first Persian national to rule since the Arabs had conquered in 641, and the first of three brilliant shahs; he was followed by Tahmasp and Abbas. It is apparent that the Safavid shahs considered rugs to be on quite a different level than their predecessors, and the rugs produced under the direction of their vision far surpassed anything woven before.

Rug weaving began to be patronized as an art just as painting or book making had been, and artists were hired to produce cartoons for the weavers. Shah Abbas set up rug ateliers or factories under his supervision in Kashan and Ispahan. Their rugs managed to combine the delicacy found in later rugs with energy and vigorous color. They were harmonious but not flashy, fine but not faddish or decadent. It was also during this period that national pride in this unique product began to mount, and the interest of foreigners grew as much as it was encouraged. Shah Tahmasp wrote to Sultan Suleiman in Baghdad offering him carpets for the mosque he was having built in Istanbul, and Shah Abbas presumably had the "Polonaise" rugs made in his workrooms for King Sigismund I.

Ironically, it could be said that the Safavid shahs took the artistic elements left behind by 1000 years of foreign invasion—the cartouches and borders from China, the Arabic writing style, the medallion and jungle ideas from the Mongol book, the tree of life, and all the diverse elements that give the rugs their richness—and adapted them to create rugs that have never been equaled. They developed the hunting rug, the garden rug, and the vase rug, the last of which provided the model for the classic Persian rug type as we know it. For after all what is a Persian rug but flowers of every size, shape, and color sprayed across an incredibly fine pile. This abstract surface that began with realistic representation was a direct outgrowth of the work of centuries of weavers of the finest brocades and velvets and painters of tiny miniatures. The use of the materials was exquisite and the fineness of texture a result of the use of the wool of sheep bred for this purpose, or the addition of gold, silver, or silk threads.

In 1722 the Safavid Dynasty surrendered to the Afghans. Later the Afshahari tribe and the Qajars each ruled for relatively short periods until Reza Khan, the first Pahlavi, took control in 1926. By the mid-nineteenth century a substantial rug trade with the West had been established, and for a considerable period rug weaving was the main industry of Persia. Many Western firms sent staffs of agents to cities like Kirman and Tabriz that exported thousands of rugs a year in order to ensure a salable product. They bought the wool, had it dyed in colors popular in the West, sold it to the weavers, dictated the size of the rug, and made designs exclusively for the Western market, such as the Sarouk in Plate 15. They even oversaw the factories. In fact, they did everything but knot the rugs.

Like the Sarouk, considered a classic, many of these products are superb rugs. As a rule, they are recognizable as rugs made for the Western market, but it takes a bit of experience in the marketplace to identify one. One's preference is a matter of taste. There are Western consumers who insist on "more authenticity," but on the other hand these rugs are now sought after by Middle Easterners interested in buying back their native products.

During World War I most of these Western businessmen fled. They did not return after the war because the feeling of nationalism in Persia was so high that it was no longer feasible or perhaps possible for a foreigner to exercise such autocracy.

In pandering to Western taste to such an extent, the representatives of the larger concerns learned through the decades that the Europeans preferred deeper, richer tones than the Americans, who inclined toward the lighter colors and pastels. They had very quickly established rug styles quite different from the original Persian family rugs that had been scouted out by eighteenth-century dealers. Those were designed to be laid out in groups of four. The central rug, which was the largest in the group, was called the *mian farsh* and measured 16 to 20 by 6 to 8 feet. Alongside it on both sides were identical runners, or *kenarehs,* that measured around 3 feet wide by the same width as the *mian farsh.* At one end of these three rugs was

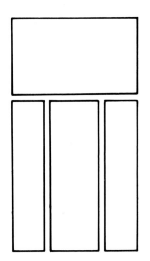

Antique rug arrangement: *Mian farsh, kenarehs,* and *kellegi*

Crab (*harshang*)

a *kellegi* whose length was the sum of the ends of the other three, which could be anywhere from 10 to 12 feet, and its width was 5 to 6 feet. The effect was decidedly Oriental. Some of the guard borders are identical, and usually the colors all fall in the same range, but at first glance the four rugs, except for the *kenarehs,* appear to be entirely independent of each other. After a time one notices that the corners of the fields, for example, have the same floral background, or the arabesques the same pattern of branching. The rugs do in fact have a kinship, but a subtle one, far more difficult to grasp aesthetically than a modern design such as a large medallion on a red field.

For that in fact is what sells in today's Persian market. The old Persian style has been changed by exposure to Western taste, but this century has also brought a new element to influence the output of the weavers: For the first time, a large class of Persians can afford their own rugs. Their preference is for highly decorated medallion styles not popular in the West but interestingly enough they do have a big market in countries around the Persian Gulf and Saudi Arabia. Many of them are made in Meshed and Tabriz.

Other Persian favorites are finely knotted new products of Ispahan, Kashan, and Nain. In state photographs the shah and shahnaz stand on rugs similar to those in Plates 7 and 8. The fine knot is a distinctly Persian characteristic, just as certain design motifs, like paisley, are distinctly Persian. They are used repeatedly in various combinations, their shapes experimented with endlessly. These familiar forms, while they might have indigenous or traditional meanings, are not symbolic to their weavers. It could be said that a Persian weaves a rug with a tree on it but that a rug dealer in Hamburg sells the same rug with a "tree of life" on it. Of course, from an ethnological or anthropological standpoint these symbols do have intrinsic interest, although they lost their immediate symbolism to the weavers centuries ago.

Of the specific designs, the crab is probably the easiest to recognize. It is called the *harshang* in Persia and is knotted into rugs from the Feraghan, Hamadan, and Heriz districts.

The *boteh,* a Persian word meaning "cluster of leaves," is the slanted teardrop such as that found in the corners of the Kirman in Plate 10. It could come from either the palm or the pine. It is the most popular motif in Persia and formed the basis for the paisleys that were considered to be such high fashion in the last century. In rugs they are designed with such variety that many regions, such as Serabend and Qum (Plates 14 and 9), have their own characteristic *botehs.* When knotted in straight rather than curved lines, the *boteh* takes on quite a different appearance, one that is short, fat, and friendly rather than graceful and womblike. An example of this variety is seen in the Sehna flat weave in Plate 18. Various types are woven into the rugs of Tabriz, Kashan, Sehna, Qainat, Kirman, Qum, and the Caucasus. Serabend uses only the *boteh,* to the exclusion of other decoration.

The *herati* design, thought to be from Herat, is a rosette encircled by two leaves. Generally speaking, the leaves are asymmetrical to the borders of the rug. Sometimes there are four leaves around the rosette. The leaves originated as fish, and in Persia

Botehs

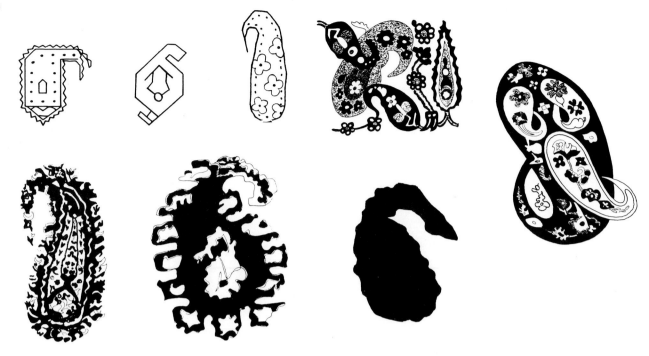

they are still called *mahi*, or fish. Looking at the Feraghan in Plate 4, it is evident that the focus of this design, rather than the rosette, can be the diamond shape formed by the backs of the leaves.

The *herati* is often used to cover the whole field. Alternatively, it is used in a border pattern combined with the "turtle," as may be seen in Plates 15 and 17 (from Sarouk and Sehna) and 89 (from India). It is found in rugs from almost every province—Arak, Feraghan, Hamadan, Sehna, Tabriz, Meshed, the Qainat, Yezd, Bijar, Heriz, and the tribes of Fars and Beluchi. A plant called *gul-henna*, or *gol henai*, from which henna is extracted, is often used as background in Abbasid designs. From a straight stalk come numerous parallel budding stems at an angle. The *gol henai* is highly stylized, the straight lines contrasting attractively with the more extravagant flowers. It is used in Mushkabad, Mahal, Arak, and Sultanabad.

Herati

Herati style used in border   Detail

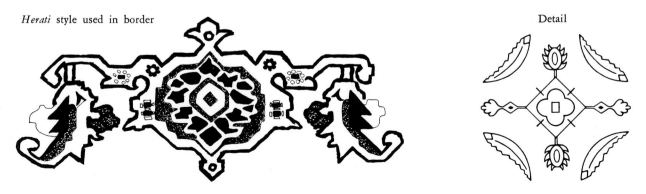

Gol henai

Mina Khani, antique and modern interpretations

Antique

Modern Detail

Bid majnum, or weeping willow

Aside from these small specific decorations, there are large overall designs that have almost become conventions, like the medallion. The medallion is complemented by designs similar to it in the corners of the field, a practice called *lecheh torunj.* The idea was probably taken from the tooled leather book covers of the fifteenth century, where it is often seen, though on a much smaller scale. Medallion rugs have been woven in almost every urban weaving area.

The Mina Khani is named after the great builder from Tabriz who was the sister of a forgotten Khan (*khani* is the feminine form of *khan*). It is an all-over pattern consisting of circles and arcs that lends a rhythmic dynamism to the whole rug. Like the *herati,* it may be seen from several angles, using different elements as focus. The Mushkabad carpets of Arak, Tabriz, Heriz, Hamadan, Chahan, and Mahal use it extensively.

One of the most memorable rug prototypes is the Shah Abbas, also known as the vase design. Like the Mina Khani, it is an all-over design. The vase is emblematic, but the flowers stemming from it cover the rug as if strung on a net. These large rugs are made in Kirman, Kashan, Tabriz, Ispahan, and Meshed, all urban rug-weaving centers.

All-over design

One antique motif that originated as a rural design and has become a favorite of the cities in the twentieth century is the weeping willow, or *bid majnun.* In its stylized form two branches arch away from the top of a tree trunk, with flowers or leaves suggested at the ends of the stalks. The weeping willow was a standard component of the ancient garden rug, which was rather like a checkerboard on which each square displayed a kind of flower. This format may vary, but it is always divided into squares or triangles containing foliage. Some of the most beautiful garden rugs, like the McMullan in the Metropolitan, may be seen in museums. The new Bakhtiari in this collection (Plate 1) is rather like a poor man's version of a garden rug. The weeping willow as the central motif has been found in rugs from Bijar, Hamadan, Arak, and Malayer. In this century it has served as the basis for a new style called the meditation rug, which is a rectangle with a slightly curved arch at the top of one end of the field. It is reminiscent of a prayer rug, but the arch is softer. Meditation rugs were first devised with a weeping willow forming the basis for the arch, filled in with greenery and birds.

Aside from these characteristic designs so often seen in Persian rugs, birds and animals are often seen, such as the eagle, peacock, ram, hare, horse, elephant, camel, lion, leopard, tiger, gazelle, ibex, griffin, sphinx, dragon, and phoenix. Flowers include the lotus, tulip, dianthus, hyacinth, and cypress. Not surprisingly, there are several other odd lots of ornaments—the Chinese cloudband and rosette, for example. One of the most interesting facets of Persian rugs is that they often depict men. Because their knotting was so fine, these could be fairly close likenesses of a patron, for example, or a shah.

TYPICAL PERSIAN
RUG DECORATIONS

The pomegranate

The tree of life

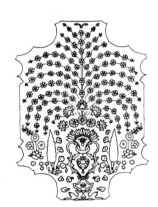

Vase patterns

Cypress

Flower arrangements

Rosette

The cloudband, a Chinese pattern

Borders

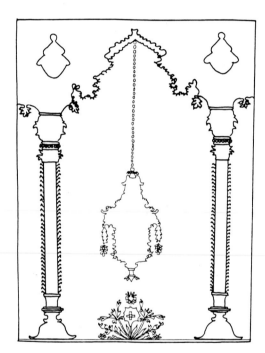

Persian prayer rug, outline of interior design

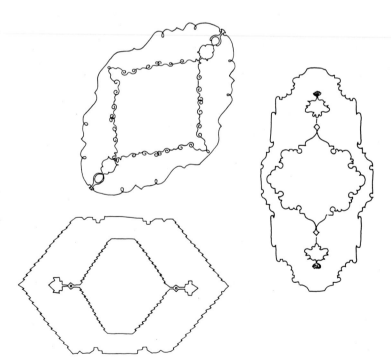

Some field interiors

1. BAKHTIARI

ca. 1930, 6' × 4'9" [m. 1.85 × 1.48]
Warp: wool
Weft: wool, two shoots after each row of knots
Knotting: Ghiordes, wool, 56 knots per square inch
[900 per dm.²]

Bakhtiari is the name of a great tribe, a branch of which has settled in Shahr Kurd in central Persia (which is, incidentally, the birthplace of Soraya Pahlavi).

The production of Bakhtiaris dates back only to the period between the two world wars. Some fairly good rugs were produced, those known as Bakhtiari Bibibaff, that is, with a knot (*baff*) in the fine tradition of a Bakhtiari princess named Bibi. The most common design is shown here: floral motifs enclosed in small frames, either linear or in the form of a trellis. In one respect the product of Bakhtiari, modern as it is, is very unusual. This is one of the last places where the colors are made from the old vegetable dyes. The colors are primitive, honest, true, and will last forever. In this example the true red border and red throughout the squares is contrasted with green, blue, white, and many other colors.

Today the trade name Bakhtiari designates a large production from the area woven by Turks, Kurds, and Armenians, which accounts for the use of both Sehna and Ghiordes knots. Unfortunately, they are not sufficiently fine to qualify as good investments.

2. BALUCHISTAN

mid-19th century, 11′ × 6′8″ [m. 3.40 × 2.06]
Warp: wool
Weft: wool, two shoots after each row of knots
Knotting: Sehna, wool, 80 knots per square inch [1280 per dm.²]

Baluchistan is a trade name denoting rugs woven by the Baluchi tribes of Khorassan on the eastern border of Persia. The Baluchi weavings are influenced by those of their neighbors, the Turkoman tribes. Consequently, dark, reddish colors and an accentuated geometric design are present, in contrast to the lighter colors and curvilinear design of other Khorassan rugs.

Because of its individuality, this Baluchi is of unique quality. Like the rug in Plate 98, it is composed mainly of brown and blue. But while the Chinese rug is uncluttered and serene and uses the brown to accentuate the several shades of bright blue, the Baluchistan appears shaggy, worn, and primitive. The Baluchistan uses one blue to set off at least five shades of brown, from dark brown to red brown to a pale tea color.

The field is decorated by medallions very similar to the "elephant's foot" of the Turkomans (Plates 87 and 88), also noticed in the Caucasian flat-weave Soumak in Plate 77. Each is decorated with what looks like a string of arrows, an old Chinese motif. The rosetted flowers connected by rows of pushpins, called the "tree of life," are reminiscent of a design from Samarkand that was used in very old garden rugs. The inside border is a version of the popular wineglass-and-leaf border. Adjacent is a variation of the Chinese endless knot, and beside it are the tiny stars found in so many Caucasian borders. The large central border is another version of the elephant's foot.

This is a very large nomadic rug and is unusually red for a Baluchistan. The tree of life, seen everywhere behind the elephant's feet in the field, is rare and lends homogeneity and dynamism to the whole. But perhaps the most unusual aspect of this rug is that at each end there is a rather long section of *kilim* rather than the usual few rows of flat weave.

Modern Baluchi rugs are small, inexpensive, and monotonously colored.

3. BIJAR

19th century, 7'3″ × 4'6″ [m. 2.18 × 1.42]
Warp: cotton
Weft: cotton, two shoots after each row of knots
Knotting: Sehna, wool, 272 knots per square inch [4350 per dm.²]

Bijar is a Kurdish town ini northwestern Persia. Its once-flourishing production has been almost extinct since World War II.

Older Bijars were knotted on a foundation of heavy woolen warps, and as many as five weft threads were passed between each row of knots. This made the rugs so rigid that they were sometimes impossible to fold. The few lighter pieces made were named Halvaï Bijars after a soft Oriental cake called *halvà.* The warp was often wool, a live fiber subject to alteration. This and the technical nature of Bijar looms were the cause of frequent irregularity of proportion.

The decoration of the field is inconsistent, and a common denominator is to be traced only in the border, which generally carries a floral stylization originating in the city of Herat; since it reminds one of a turtle, it is referred to in the trade as the *herati* turtle border.

This particular field is decorated with stylized roses like the ones seen in the Karabagh, a district in the Caucasus (see Plate 44). It is a more realistic design than is commonly found in Persian rugs. It has a certain similarity in its softness of color and use of the *herati* motif to the Indian rug in Plate 89.

Were it not woven by a master, the color in this piece could be quite garish—pale blue, pink, and red on dark blue is hardly a refined color scheme. But much of the blue has streaked white, and the colors, rather than glaring, are mellow and harmonious.

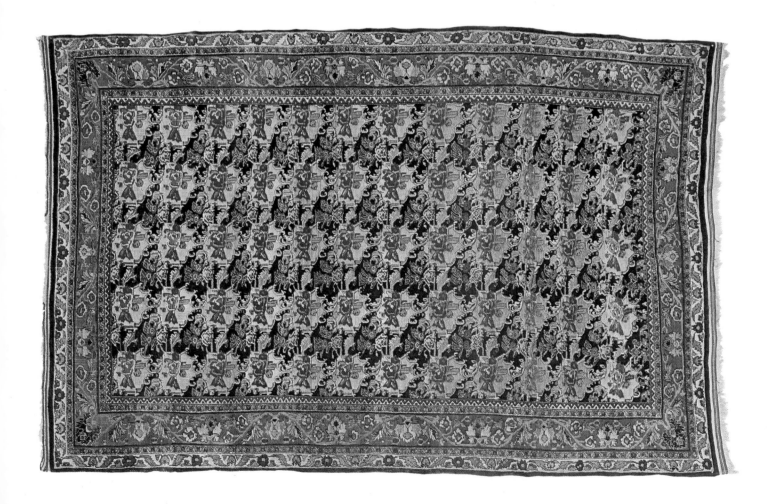

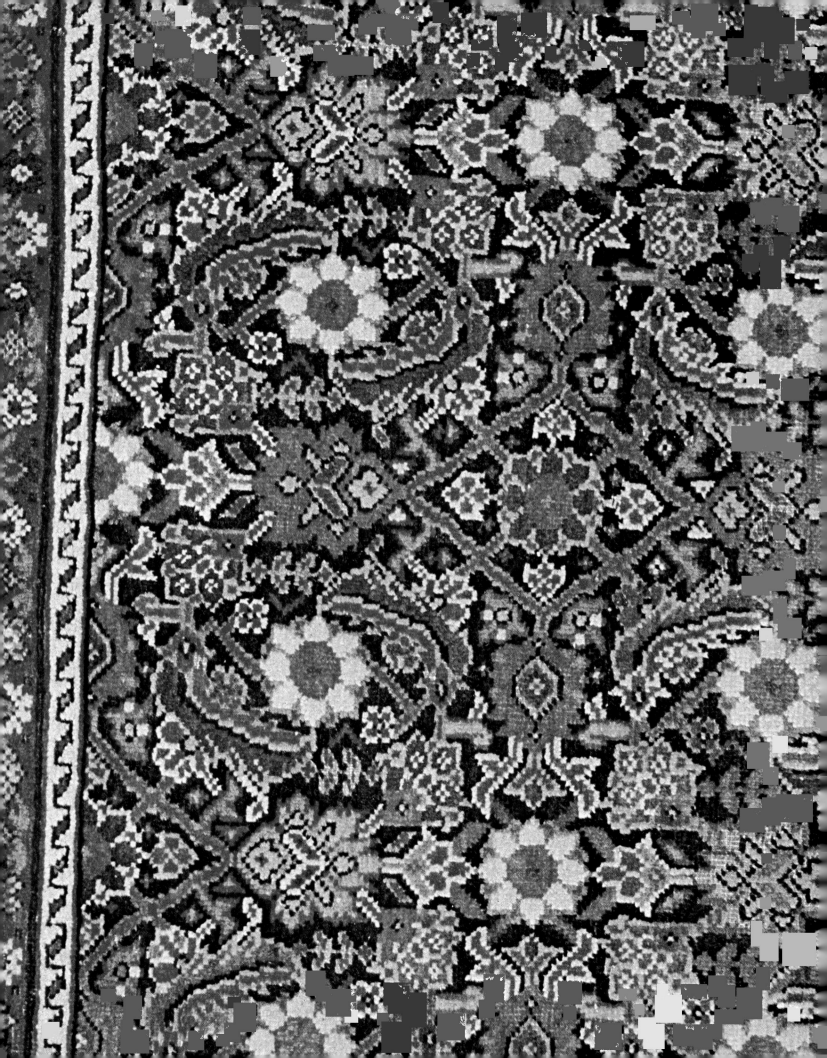

4. FERAGHAN

early 19th century, 6'2" × 4'2" [m. 1.90 × 1.30]
Warp: cotton
Weft: cotton, two shoots after each row of knots
Knotting: Sehna, wool, 132 knots per square inch [950 per dm.²]

Feraghan is the name of a district in west-central Persia north of the city of Sarouk. Rug weaving started here in the late eighteenth century and is contemporary with the introduction of the designs originating in Herat, mentioned in Plate 3. Because of Feraghan's large production for export to Europe and particularly to England, these rugs are well known to Westerners.

This design typifies the Persian tradition of flowers, the *herati* motif and the thick, dense all-over pattern in many different colors, bordered by five distinct rows breaking up the pattern even more.

About 90 percent of all Feraghans have an all-over *herati* field and turtle borders. An interesting aspect of the *herati* motif, the rosette with two leaves offsetting it, is that it is not a symmetrical north-south-east-west design. In this rug it is clearly the dominant motif, yet it is lined up on the diagonal, and the borders cut off the design arbitrarily. Although at first the sides of the rug appear to be identical, when one looks carefully at the three white diamond shapes right across the center of the rug it is evident that they are not. The rug is organized by lines of flowers forming squares around each *herati*. At the corners of the squares are diamond shapes that indicate the direction of a very loose arabesque that runs through the rug in yet another all-over design. In this rug one sees why Persian rugs are considered to be complex.

Twentieth-century Feraghan production deals mainly with long and narrow formats (runners and "kelleys" 12 to 16 feet long by 5 to 7 feet wide). The fact that these formats are rarely adaptable to Western interiors makes Feraghans relatively inexpensive, although of good value.

5. HAMADAN

ca. 1920, 11′8″ × 3′8″ [m. 3.60 × 1.15]
Warp: wool
Weft: wool, two to three shoots after each row of knots
Knotting: Ghiordes, wool, 80 knots per square inch
  [1280 per dm.²]

Hamadan is a district and town in north-central Persia. The name embraces a large number of rugs produced in the area or marketed through the town, generally inexpensive if not mediocre. The use of camel wool in its natural color on runners brought these rugs wide acceptance in Europe, where long, dark nineteenth century corridors were lightened by their soft beige tones. Not surprisingly, when color is used, usually poor-quality synthetic indigo, these rugs' worst qualities betray themselves. Hamadans sometimes employ as many as four warp threads, and they are also identifiable by a peculiar horizontal weft stripe that runs on the back of the rug and reveals the sparseness of their knotting. Their design often shows a hexagon in the middle of a field of smaller figures, or a number of hexagons in runners.

Among Hamadans, pieces knotted for the weaver's own use and not for export are by far the best rugs, and in fact the simplicity of the rug in Plate 5 indicates a nomadic origin. It is camel-colored, with touches of red, black, and white. The outside border is decorated by birds and diamonds filled with hooks, motifs seen in the Caucasus and parts of Turkey. In the border there are also designs similar to the candelabra seen in prayer rugs. The two interlocking borders reverse each other. The diamonds down the center of the field are decorated with more hooks, camels, diamonds, and triangles of all kinds. At the top of the rug the weaver shows signs of not knowing how to stop, an affliction common to artists of all kinds all over the world.

6. HERIZ

19th century, 12′ × 8′7″ [m. 3.63 × 2.60]
Warp: cotton
Weft: cotton, two shoots after each row of knots
Knotting: Ghiordes, wool, 90 knots per square inch
[1440 per dm.²]

Heriz is an area in northwestern Persia south of the Caucasus that has produced some of the world's most popular rugs for a century and a half. While Heriz rugs are of high quality, rugs woven in Sarab are even finer, while those from Gorevan are coarser. Karadagh and Karadja rugs are usually runners.

Rug weaving did not start in this region until the early nineteenth century, but it gained enthusiastic acceptance almost immediately. The main reason is that Heriz decoration appropriated the geometric designs of the nearby Caucasus. Even though they are geometric, the designs are characterized by Persian delicacy.

In older rugs a large central medallion usually dominates the field and is partially reproduced in one of the four corners. Intersecting these main elements of decoration are leaves, branches, and flowers. The borders are rich, often carrying the *herati* turtle motif.

The colors vary from pale azure through pink, beige, and terracotta to deeper shades. Except for the few silk specimens, Herizes were woven in large sizes, many of which have found their way to Europe and America.

This is the first of our Persian rugs containing relatively large undecorated spaces. Here a rust medallion on a pale decorated rectangle outlined in indigo is inside a more regular rust rectangle. The two white guard borders are decorated with the standard tulip, vine, and rosette motif, and the wide dark border is filled in by the *herati* and the turtle. The dark border is affected by *abrash*, as is the body of the rug.

The high prices that older rugs of this type fetch today represent only a fraction of their real value owing to their scarcity. A beautifully preserved mid-nineteenth-century silk Heriz fetched a record price at auction when it was sold for $200,000 at Sotheby Parke Bernet in New York on February 4, 1977.

7. ISPAHAN

ca. 1955, 7'5" × 4'10" [m. 2.30 × 1.50]
Warp: silk
Weft: silk, two shoots after each row of knots
Knotting: Sehna, wool and silk, 810 knots per square
  inch [12,900 per dm.²]

Ispahan, the "Pearl of Iran," was Persia's capital until the last century. During the sixteenth century one of the court manufactures flourished there under Shah Abbas the Great. Possibly the splendid rugs he gave to various royal personages of the Western world, including the Polonaise rugs, were made there. Rug weaving was resumed in Ispahan after World War I and has produced rugs with meticulous knotting and wonderfully fine quality. The designs are floral, usually repetitions of the antique Shah Abbas motif. Natural dyes are still used.

Only a few miles east of Ispahan is the village of Nain, which set up looms just before World War II for the manufacture of the most closely knotted con-temporary rugs. Both Ispahans and Nains invariably use the Sehna knot, but the colors of Nains are colder, and to many people the perfection of their structure detracts from their charm.

The design of this rug appears sharp because it has been knotted with an extraordinary 810 knots per square inch. From it one can get an idea of what the oldest rugs were like, when the knotting was just as dense, the colors vegetable dyes, but the designs freer and more primitive.

This design is interesting. The spiraling gold lines that circle the medallion in the center are the clearest example of a multiple arabesque encircling the whole rug. In the four corners of the field are more arabesques meandering to fill a triangular space. The *botehs* are so distinct that it is easy to see why the literal translation of the word is "cluster of leaves." In the field the *botehs* are simple, in the wide border double-tailed. On the *kilim* is the inscription *Iran Ispahan, Karkhari Maamouri*, denoting the factory and the weaver's name. There is a white, green, and red border at either side, the colors of the Iranian flag.

8. KASHAN

ca. 1940, 6'10" × 4' [m. 2.10 × 1.27]
Warp: silk
Weft: silk, two shoots after each row of knots
Knotting: Sehna, silk 418 knots per square inch [6700 per dm.²]

Kashan is in the central highlands of Persia halfway between Ispahan and Teheran. Its weaving tradition dates back to the sixteenth century, when Shah Abbas I founded a court manufacture there. The rugs have maintained a high standard of quality. The Sehna knot is exquisitely rendered, and the curvilinear design is as observant of detail as a Persian miniature.

Quite a few exceptional pieces dating as far back as 1820 through 1860 are known as Montashemi after a master weaver in one of the main contemporary establishments. Modern rugs are sometimes made of *kurk* wool, which is combed from the necks of lambs in wintertime rather than sheared in springtime. The pile is cut low to enhance the details of the design, and even now there is some production in silk. It is hard to convey the real luxury of a Kashan rug.

Joshagan, a town near Kashan, also produces a finely knotted type called meditation rugs. They are designed with a large pot at the bottom from which grows a rich profusion of foliage, perhaps a weeping willow, flowers, and sometimes birds. The fronds form an arch at the top of the rug, creating the effect of a garden prayer rug. A modern, jazzy type to the traditionalists in the rug business, they are actually quite appealing, often woven in silk of the softest colors.

The odd silk Kashan in Plate 8 is unusual for the tartness of its red and blue decorations and its use of contrast. Red, blue, and the cream background are common in Kashans, as is the central medallion composed of three superimposed medallions. As in Plate 7, the extensive arabesque encircling the medallions is in the form of a vine, here green. It provides the basis for the all-over flower design and, while not as easy to follow as the gold one in Plate 7, is actually more necessary to the whole scheme.

9. KIRMAN

mid-19th century, 6'11" × 4'4" [m. 2.12 × 1.38]
Warp: cotton
Weft: cotton, two shoots after each row of knots
Knotting: Sehna, wool, 240 knots per square inch [3850 per dm.²]

Kirman is a major rug-producing area in southeastern Persia. Laver (actually Ravar) has produced some of the best examples of the Kirman type, and Yezd, 250 miles northwest, wove such similar rugs that they are known as Kirman Yezd.

Certain sixteenth-century rugs identified as Southern Persian were probably woven in the Kirman area, but only since 1800 has it become the largest exporter of Persian rugs for Western use. Kirman was one of the first cities where Western agents made a large-scale industry of carpet weaving. Nineteenth-century eski ("old") Kirmans are of unparalleled beauty, and twentieth-century production has been prolific and commercially successful. Today Kirman produces thousands of rugs a year, most of which are exported to Europe and the United States. It can be argued that they are more Western than Eastern; the influence of the buyer has dictated the output of the artisan. This applies particularly to one type exported to the United States since the early Thirties: It has an undecorated light green, ivory, and azure background incompatible with the Persian predilection for detail and strong color. The lack of borders also violates one of the tenets of Persian design. An unusually high pile is requested by the Western Kirman consumer to convey a sense of softness and luxury, in contrast to the short pile that Persians prefer.

Plate 9, a "picture rug," is the first of two rugs from the Kirman area. Because of the Mohammedan taboo against artistic representation of animal and human figures, picture rugs were either commissioned by nonbelievers or knotted by them. This piece abounds with representations of human and animal figures. It illustrates the legend of Bahram, a king who loved nature, and the shepherd. Here one sees a goatherd, dogs, ducks, fish, a deer, a wolf, birds and a dog. The Arabic in the border recites a lengthy but irrelevant poem.

10. KIRMAN LAVER

mid-19th century, 8'6" × 4'7" (m. 2.64 × 1.42]
Warp: cotton
Weft: cotton, two shoots after each row of knots
Knotting: Sehna, wool, 224 knots per square inch
   [3330 per dm.²]

This exceedingly rare rug represents pure, original Eastern art. Its use of the *boteh* is unique. Although delicate,
the rug lacks the insipid quality common to Kirmans.
Each corner contains an enormous *boteh*, which, in turn,
frames another. The wide border is a series of *botehs*
connected as if in a chain. The *boteh* is ordinarily part
of a repetitive design and is used to focus a design as
it is used here. The medallion in the center is rather
ambiguously modern, being relatively undecorated and
streamlined, having few colors and such abstract decoration that no flower or derivative is easily recognized.
The field outside the medallion is only a shade different
in color and is covered with a pulsating all-over flower
design organized by an arabesque.

   In the middle of the two long borders is a fish. Fish
are rarely seen in any but picture rugs, the borders of
old Kashans, or an original garden rug. The outside and
inside borders and the two red borders are identical.
The outside border is a reverse border typical of Persia,
and the red border is the flower and vine seen all
through the rug-producing countries.

11. KURDISTAN NOMAD RUG

late 19th century, 13'3" × 3'1" [m. 4.10 × 0.96]
Warp: wool
Weft: wool, two shoots after each row of knots
Knotting: Ghiordes, wool, 63 knots per square inch
[1010 per dm.²]

Kurdistan is a large, relatively nomadic district in western Persia. Mosul, an oil city now under the jurisdiction of Iraq, was probably once a transit town for the local rugs and those of the Hamadan area on their way to Turkish market harbors. In this sense Mosul is a misnomer, as it is not indicative of the origin of the rugs it names. While the use of a single weft thread and four warps helps us identify many Hamadans, there are actually no yardsticks to identify Mosuls other than the general characteristics of coarse knotting, inferior wool, and poor dye. Rugs made by the Kurdish nomadic tribes, however, may have a marvelous primitive vigor. Today there is a tendency to reevaluate the naive boldness of rugs woven by these pastoral tribes for their own use. They are at the very least original.

It is interesting to compare this rug with Caucasian pieces such as those in Plates 37 and 65 with Persian ones such as that in Plate 5 and with the Turkish Kilim in Plate 32. This, like a Baku, has a stripe in the border for each color in the field, and like so many nomadic runners it is decorated by three diamonds running down the center.

In the field are two women, two men, and a disembodied pair of legs. There are many four-legged creatures as well, many simple trees of life, *botehs*, and a few birds at the top.

The two narrow borders are composed of rosettes and leaves, while an interesting extra strip at the bottom has rosettes and leaves spaced in such a way as to be similar to certain Navaho designs.

The field is a red with brown in it characteristic of nomads, set off by blue, brown, and white designs. The central medallion is navy, the other two shades of white or cream tinted by the red of the field.

12. MAHAL

19th century, 11'2" × 9'1" [m. 3.40 × 2.77]
Warp: wool
Weft: wool
Knotting: Sehna
From the collection of Mr. Vojtech Blau

The province of Arak-Ajeni is famous for its stupendous output of attractive commercial rugs. Hamadan, the Plain of Feraghan, Mirabad, Sarouk, Arak, and Qum cluster together in the south, their proximity no doubt stimulating competition. Except for Hamadans and Serabends, most of the carpets from this area were produced expressly for the West.

Arak, the capital, was founded as Sultanabad by Fath Ali Shah. After the middle of the nineteenth century it became a leading producer of factory rugs and was dominated by European and American houses. In the twentieth century its output has ceased almost completely, but at one time Arak and the surrounding villages could produce hundreds of rugs a month. They are called Sultanabads, Mahals, and Savalans. Most are room-sized, and they are often coarsely woven. The Muskabads to the northwest are quite similar to the Mahals.

This extravagant piece was made for the house of Ziegler in Germany. Ziegler was one of the fine European importers who stationed agents in the Middle East in order to ensure the production of rugs that would be popular in their markets. At first glance the design is not composed of the classic arabesques one expects of a large Persian factory rug, but this is a misperception. It is actually a variation on the vase rug, but the centers of the large, rather languorous arabesques have been filled with color rather than flowers. This clarifies the lines of the arabesque, which is usually disguised by the flowers and other elements of the design.

The border is also a languorous but rich *herati* guarded by several narrower borders. The primary color in the field is red. The vases are light brown streaked and lightened by *abrash*, and the background ranges from navy to lighter blues also streaked by *abrash*.

13. KHORASSAN—MESHED

ca. 1920, 6'2" × 3'11" [m. 1.90 × 1.22]
Warp: cotton
Weft: cotton, two shoots after each row of knots
Knotting: Sehna, wool, 182 knots per square inch [2900 per dm.²]

Khorassan is the extreme northeast province of Persia. Its capital is Meshed, where, oddly enough, rugs are woven in both the Sehna and Ghiordes knots. The latter, when used in Meshed, identifies the rug as Turkbaff ("Turkish knot").

A peculiarity of rugs woven in this region is the use of a soft, lustrous wool of inimitable brilliance. The pile is cut at medium height. The pattern, less clear than that of a Kashan or a Nain, is more pleasant to some people.

This rug reminds one of a childhood birthday joke—placing a small gift in a series of increasingly larger boxes and wrapping them all individually. The Persians treat the arabesque medallions in their rugs in somewhat the same way. Inside the rectangular border is a large and showy medallion enclosing a somewhat smaller and less pretentious one, until at the center there is a peony, the *vajra* star, or the simplest of diamonds (in this case, a rosette).

Aside from the fact that this rug is an example of the Persian preoccupation with medallions, it is also characteristic in its handling of the field. Each arabesque is concluded at its points by a flower in the field outside it, forcing it open and connecting it to the whole. A large flower is in each of the four corners, and two narrow guard borders of the reverse flower and leaf frame a wider, more complex flower-and-leaf border. The field is alternately blue and red, dictated by the arabesque.

The medallion and arabesque are interesting to compare with those in Plates, 7, 8, 15, 21, and 22. And for the sake of contrast, the Baluchistan in Plate 2 was made in the same province.

14. QUM

ca. 1955, 6′10″ × 3′6″ [m. 2.12 × 1.40]
Warp: cotton
Weft: cotton, two shoots after each row of knots
Knotting: Sehna, wool, 195 knots per square inch [3100 per dm.²]

Qum (pronounced "goom" by Persians) is a town in central Persia approximately 90 miles south of Teheran. Although rug weaving did not start there earlier than the 1930s, it has gained a reputation for finely knotted modern rugs. Unfortunately, it has no tradition of its own but simply borrows designs here and there.

A few silk flowers in a rug is enough for a Qum to be designated as wool *and* silk. The buyer must be alert to this practice.

Plate 14 is an interesting example of the *boteh* and should be compared with the Sehna in Plate 16, the Serabend in Plate 19, and the Baku from the Caucasus in Plate 40. While the Sehna and the Serabend are elegant old antiques, the colors worn and the shape well defined, the Qum is young, fresh, and bright, with a less well defined, fat and friendly *boteh*. The use of pastels—blue, white, beiges, and pink, offset by only a touch of red—identifies it as intended for the Western market.

15. SAROUK

late 19th century, 7'3" × 4'3" [m. 2.24 × 1.30]
Warp: cotton
Weft: cotton, two shoots after each row of knots
Knotting: Sehna, wool, 210 knots per square inch [3300
   per dm.²]

Sarouk is a village near Arak (Sultanabad) where the weaving of this extremely pleasant type of rug originated in the 1850s. Although the designs are reminiscent of those of certain Kashans, Sarouks nevertheless stand on their own and command high prices.

Most often, a medallion of large proportions is inscribed on a red or blue background, oval or round in shape, and is extended by pointed floral designs toward the fringed ends.

The older Sarouks invariably used light pink or other pastel colors. They are as expensive as they are attrac-tive. But even the maroon variety that found its way to the United States in the period between the two world wars has been able to multiply its original price many times. This type is now in demand by the German market.

This is one of the most satisfying commercial rugs in this book from both the aesthetic and the traditional points of view. It is strong and supple and clearly shows each nuance of design. It is designed in the traditional "medallion inside medallion" style, with an arabesque defining the points of the central dark blue medallion and arabesques of flowers encircling each medallion. Two guard borders are on either side of a wide border with the *herati* motif. Two factors distinguish this rug from the 1001 Persian rugs similar to it: First, the color is clear and used well in terms of contrast, and second, the shape of the medallion is somewhat more angular and better defined than most, having real right angles and points.

16. SEHNA

19th century, 5'10" × 4'2" [m. 1.80 × 1.28]
Warp: cotton
Weft: cotton, one shoot after each row of knots
Knotting: Ghiordes, wool, 223 knots per square inch
    [3500 per dm.²]

Sehna is the city in the region of Kurdistan that gave its name to the Persian technique of knotting although, as already mentioned, the Turkish knot is used in the town itself.

The best Sehnas have a refinement and originality unsurpassed by any other Persian weave. Sehnas also have a unique texture. The workmanship has not changed in 200 years.

The most exquisite pieces come only from the town of Sehna itself. They are sometimes woven on a silk warp, and the density of knotting is particularly fine. The pile is cut short. The main designs used are either a hexagonal central medallion or a colored background filled with small flowers or rows of *botehs*.

Rugs woven in Sehna designs by nomadic tribes outside the city are only a little less refined and are known in the trade as Sehna-Kurds.

This is probably the original *boteh*, as it comes from a city where weaving has been practiced for so many years and where the field of *botehs* is one of the most often used and traditional designs. It is thought that the design stems from a "cluster of leaves," and this translation makes it clear that the design incorporates several leaves and blossoms on a single stem.

Although it is a nineteenth-century piece, this rug follows the old tradition of identical guard borders on either side of a wider border and a loose interpretation of the *herati* motif in the wide border. In this case the dark border (black background) makes a fine contrast to the cream color of the field, set off by tones of pale green and pink in the design, outlined in black. *Abrash* is seen at the base of the field, particularly in the green of the leaves atop the *boteh*.

This rug is distinguished by the beauty of a silk bell-pull that has faded from carmine to rose: soft, refined, yet vibrant.

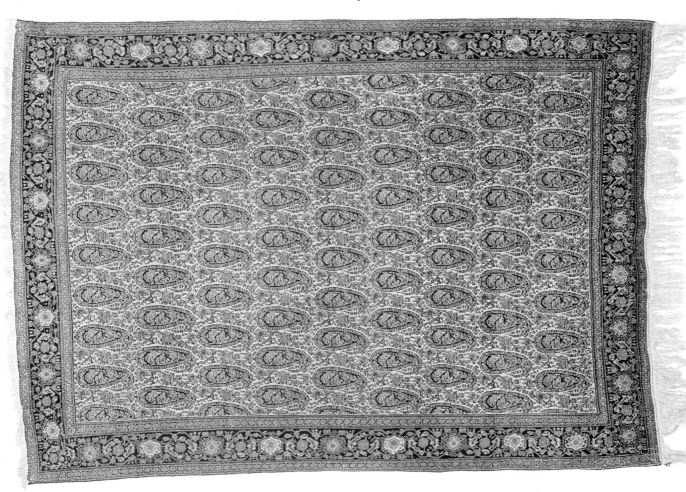

17. SEHNA

mid-19th century, 6'2" × 4'4" [m. 1.90 × 1.36]
Warp: cotton
Weft: cotton, two shoots after each row of knots
Knotting: Ghiordes, wool, 169 knots per square inch
[2700 per dm.²]

This is just as much a classic Sehna as the rug in Plate 16. A bit of the angularity that distinguishes Sarouks (to which this type has often been compared; see Plate 15) is evident, but the field here is much less crowded with flowers and the medallions have six straight sides rather than curves. The edges are in some cases serrated, as in the diagonal outside edges of the large and small six-sided figures. Like that in Plate 16, the border consists of two identical narrow guard borders and a wider one containing the *herati* motif.

An interesting comparison may also be made to certain floral designs found in the Karabagh in Plate 42 and the Sejshour in Plate 55. Although they do not appear to be floral, on closer inspection one sees that each motif is a stylized flower.

The color contrast here has as much bite as the serrated edges. The wide outside border is a deep red. The central medallion is white, the secondary one red, the tertiary one white, and on the outside a black background is employed.

18. SEHNA KILIM

19th century, 4'11" × 3'10" [m. 1.52 × 1.18]
Warp: wool
Knotting: flat weave, pile wool

Sehna artisans produce a flat-woven double-faced Kilim, among the finest of that weave in Persia. These rugs are unusually strong and supple. As previously mentioned, the nature of the weaving technique dictates angularity of design, and it may be seen that this repeated field is composed of rosettes and the *herati* motif. The small borders are leaf and vine, the large ones angular *botehs.* This particular example is extraordinary by virtue of its rarity, technical superiority, and good state of preservation.

The color scheme is quite similar to that of the rug in Plate 16—pink, green, and black on a dominant cream background. Here the central border is yellow, the two outside it red.

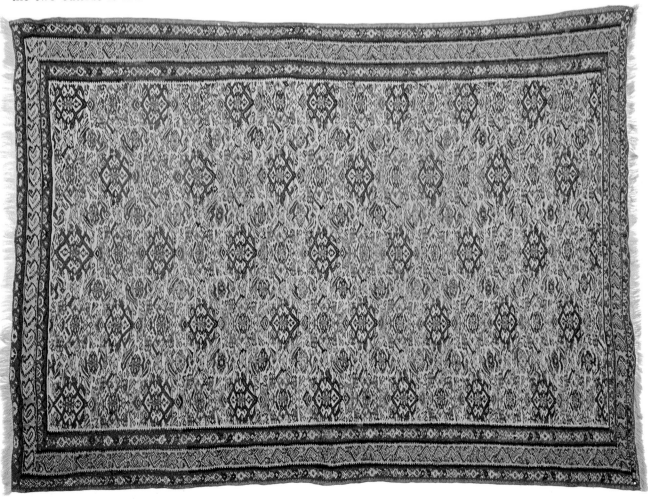

19. SERABEND

19th century, 7'9" × 3'3" ([m. 2.40 × 1.30]
Warp: cotton
Weft: cotton, one shoot after each row of knots
Knotting: Ghiordes, wool, 120 knots per square inch
[1900 per dm.²]

Serabend is a mountainous district west of Sultanabad. Mir—the name of a village or of an elite class—is synonymous in the trade with the finer nineteenth or early-twentieth-century Serabends.

A particular design identifies these rugs: the *boteh* or palmette or Kashmir pear. It invariably appears on the coarser Serabend runners. The same motif, with the horizontal lines of *botehs* alternately pointing right and left, identifies Mirs. Usually they are of the "kelley" format.

While Serabends offer good use for their modest price, Mirs are also sought out. Europeans are particularly appreciative of their sober taste and their distinctiveness.

It is easy to see the individuality of this *boteh* compared with the Sehna *boteh* in Plate 16 and the Qum in Plate 14. In its unassuming repetitive design is a hint of calico, just a suggestion, which will be seen several more times in rugs from the Caucasus.

The dominant color of Serabends is red. Here the background is a faded rose; the flowers depicted in the *boteh* and the main border are red; and the *boteh* is cream with minor accents in blue and black.

20. SHIRAZ

late 19th century, 8'11" × 5' [m. 2.78 × 1.55]
Warp: wool
Weft: wool, two shoots after each row of knots
Knotting: Sehna, wool, 100 knots per square inch [1600 per dm.²]

Shiraz is the capital of the southern province of Fars. Although the city itself houses no looms, the name applies to rugs made in nearby villages. Kashgai tribesmen live in the surrounding area; Afshar tribesmen range farther east toward Kirman, and their rugs are often classified as Kirmans.

The province of Fars lies hundreds of miles south of the Caucasus, but its designs are highly reminiscent of Caucasian decoration. It has long been thought that the tribe was originally Caucasian and that a Shah Abbasid moved it to southern Persia, which would account for its idiosyncratic rugs. The field is adorned with one or many geometric medallions, contoured by stylized animals in the Caucasian manner. But these rugs have heavy brown woolen warps that show up in dark fringes, as opposed to the lighter warp generally used in Caucasian rugs.

Kashgai rugs may be identified by the many small octagons in the field, which look like circles. There are two characteristic Kashgai rug types. This type shows an affinity to those in Plates 71, 48, and 47, though Caucasian colors would be brighter than these blues and reds, which almost look washed. This color, characteristic of Kashgai products, is called red wine or red ink. In the Caucasus the background would contain similar octagons or polygons, but the flowers in the lower corners would be more geometric.

The insignia in the diamonds seems to be a corruption of the swastika that appears in every primitive culture. But this swastika is closer to Arabic script than the swastika in the Caucasian cloudband in, for example, Plate 47. And except for the crenellated edge found throughout the Caucasus, the borders are typically Persian, particularly the *boteh* border. The offshoots between the three large triangles are somewhat like the Caucasian rams' heads in Plates 50 and 52. The background is a typically crowded Persian treatment.

21. TABRIZ

19th century, 13'10" × 7' [m. 3.18 × 2.11]
Warp: cotton
Weft: cotton, two shoots after each row of knots
Knotting: Sehna, wool, 240 knots per square inch [3800 per dm.²]

Tabriz has been synonymous with a tradition of fine antiques to the Western market for centuries. Most sixteenth-century museum rugs from northwestern Persia were probably woven in Tabriz. Later, in the second half of the nineteenth century, merchants from Tabriz organized weavers all over Persia when the town's production no longer sufficed to meet the demand. In no other area is there such a clear distinction between old and new production.

Nineteenth-century weavings are identifiable by a back almost as rigid as leather owing to the waters used in dyeing the wools. These rugs are closely knotted, and they use mellow colors ranging through red, brown, and cream.

Contemporary production in Tabriz is usually coarse. But the design of the coarse rugs as well as the finer ones is dictated by Western taste. In fact, a dealer can not only tell the difference between an American and a European Tabriz but also between those woven for two neighboring countries such as Austria and Italy.

A late nineteenth-century silk Tabriz was sold at auction at Sotheby Parke Bernet for $42,000 on December, 1, 1973. The silk rugs, from Ispahan and Nain as well as Tabriz, have undoubtedly captured some of the best prices in the market for the past couple of decades, but there are other collector's items from Tabriz: the works of Hajji Djalil, a master weaver of nearby Marand. His style is ornate, and the pieces are often signed.

This particular type is one of the most popular Tabriz rugs. The unadorned field is red and the other decoration cream, with floral designs delicately sketched. The medallions, of which there are actually four, are a series of arabesques, and the floral delineation in part echoes the red in the field. The harmonies in the rug are simple and undemanding.

22. TEHERAN

ca. 1930, 6′9″ × 4′6″ [m. 2.10 × 1.40]

Warp: cotton
Weft: cotton, two shoots after each row of knots
Knotting: Sehna, wool, 234 knots per square inch [3700 per dm.²]

Teheran is the capital of Persia. Rug weaving began there during the twentieth century, mostly in surrounding villages, and only lasted until World War II.

Among cities that have entered the field recently, Teheran is one of the few that have produced a fine original rug type. Although its small meditation rug is similar to a prayer rug, the niche of the mosque is not a stylization at the top, as in Turkish rugs, but an arch embracing the entire field.

Teheran is one of the few places where both the Ghiordes and Sehna knots are used. The pile is cut short to display the design, and the wool is good. In this example the knotting is relatively fine, but the design is less clearly defined than those of the Ispahan which appears in Plate 7. Despite the coarser look of the Teheran, it is elegant and lyrical. It simulates the vase motif, one of the oldest and most satisfying Persian rug designs. At times the tree of life grows in it, and at other times a variety of flowers spring from it in profusion, as here. The unattached swirls in the field could be seen as partial arabesques or as a Persian off-shoot of the Chinese cloudband motif. The larger border is red, echoed by the medallions in the field. The background is white, and the other colors used are green, blue, black outlines, pink, gold, and yellow.

The most common field of the meditation rug is a willow whose branches form the design of the arch.

When not using the meditation pattern, the weavers in Teheran relied on graceful old designs, and the rugs are always rather small.

A help in identifying this recent but already extinct production is the frequent use of the *medachyl*, the small borders that appear as reciprocal lances or serrated edges.

TURKEY

TURKISH RUGS, like their weavers, have gained immeasurably from the political stability of the past four centuries, but a plethora of foreign influences from before this age remain like ghosts to color their personality. Until the Ottoman Empire united Turkey in the fifteenth century, its history was as fragmented as a stained-glass window. The rugs themselves are made with a stylistic diversity typical of no other region, alternately reflecting the expertise of the Armenians, the energy of the Kurds, the vibrant Mediterranean sun and water of the Greeks, and finally the blunt, warlike strength of the Turks. One comes to treasure this multiplicity of differences, though at first glance it is overwhelming.

Turkish rugs were the first to be imported to the West. Their clear primary colors, graceful antique design, and unique texture not only established them as a luxury from the very beginning but also found a market that has lasted for centuries. Despite their diversity, they are as distinctly Turkish as Chinese rugs are distinctly Chinese. Taken as a whole, the colors are brighter than those of Persian or Chinese rugs. In this respect they are more similar to the Caucasians, but sometimes they include an odd tone such as lavender that is never used elsewhere. Although the colors are not subtle, they are brilliantly used, and one reason for the immense popularity of Turkish rugs in the West is that while they are noticeable they are not garish. The design is also more akin to that of Caucasian rugs than to that of Persian or Chinese rugs—forceful, angular shapes are crowded together in a small field to create a moving impression of dynamic life.

Such is the Anatolian rug in its original form, and at this point a distinction must be made between "Anatolian" and "Turkish." Western Turkey is surrounded by water on three sides and is, in effect, an enormous peninsula. East of this peninsula the rugs have been so thoroughly influenced by the neighboring Persians that they could be classified as Persian. The rugs from Asia Minor are those that are considered to be classically Turkish, and from the standpoint of indigenous art they are clearly the most interesting.

Among the most unique and cherished Turkish rugs are the Anatolian prayer rugs. Most of these have a *mihrab,* or prayer arch, supported by a single clear color. Many have a hanging lamp within the arch, stylized flowers, or columns in the field supporting the arch. Each village or town weaves its own characteristic type. In places such as Ladik, Kula, and Ghiordes, the prayer rug has become such a familiar means of expression that many pieces display enormous individuality and verve. They are an astonishing example of how consistent work within a rigid structure can bring forth results of great richness, variety, and personality. What the *haiku* is in Japan and the sonnet in England the prayer rug is in Turkey. The prayer rug cannot be overemphasized, because it is in these small products, often created by a single weaver, that true artistry has manifested itself, rather than in the factory production of larger carpets woven by a group, the method that has stimulated the Persians to their highest effort.

A favorite exercise of history students is to search through the paintings of a particular era for signs of foreign cultural influence. Scholars of the European Renaissance and the American colonial period have been awarded many Ph.D.'s for the hundreds of Turkish rugs they have spied in portraits and ecclesiastical works from that time. One of the earliest is depicted in a Quattrocento fresco by Giotto in the Arena Chapel in Padua, and indeed many antique pieces were later found in churches throughout Europe. They were painted by such diverse artists as Jan Van Eyck, Memling, Gilbert Stuart, the Venetian School, and Gerard David. Sometimes a painter would paint one repeatedly, like a favorite woman—hence the soubriquets "Lotto" and "Holbein." They were painted as table coverings before they appeared on the floor. They are often seen in portraits commissioned by the subject, which is indicative of their value as status symbols.

American colonists ordered their furniture from London buyers by lot, specifying "one Turkey carpet," the size, and colors. Occasionally they included apprehensive grumblings concerning the taste of the London agent, which one suspects might have done them more harm than good.

Many of these first rugs imported to the West were of the same type. From the fifteenth and sixteenth centuries came the Holbeins and the Oushaks. The Holbein is a small rug with an all-over arabesque design inside a wide, distinctive border taken from *kufic* lettering. The two types of Oushaks were larger, room-sized rugs. The "star" has a red ground with wide-stemmed blue insignia opening out, the "medallion" a red ground with blue centers surrounded by yellow arabesques. Later several other types came from the court manufactures set up in Constantinople with the aid of Persian weavers, a gift from Shah Abbas that was supported through the reigns of Selim the Grim and Suleiman the Magnificent. These had a Persian cast, using, for example, the *herati* motif, but even so they retained a noticeably Turkish feeling. At this time also, a certain Persian floral quality crept into the designs. The Turks, being Sunnite Mohammedans, were generally severe in their avoidance of images of people, birds, fish, or animals. Whereas the focus in Persia is on the garden, here it is on abstract ex-

Ancient floral motif

pression. Designs that other geographic areas share, such as the *boteh* and the reciprocal trefoil border, are not often used here (this is equally true of the *herati*). One often sees what is called the "water design" border and latchhooks exaggerated beyond their Caucasian counterparts.

The Turkish rug stimulated demand in the West for more rugs of the Oriental variety, and as a result Turkey was the first region to industrialize weaving solely for the Western market. In the beginning this was a family effort; then it evolved into a system whereby numerous people worked on the same predesigned rug. Ironically, the Turkish rug industry never gained the critical approval enjoyed by the Persians. Even so, it has been successful commercially from its inception. At the turn of the century thousands of rugs were turned out every year until World War I. Along with this success came standardization, uniformity, and careless workmanship.

Like Persia, in the nineteenth century European merchants sent agents to Turkey to oversee all aspects of weaving from selecting the dyes and wool to making the design itself. Although European supervision produced some of the finest Persian rugs, it had limited success in Turkey with the exception of Oushak and Hereke.

Turkish rugs came to Western Europe and America before Chinese, Persian, or Caucasian rugs for the simple reason that Turkey is the westernmost point of Asia, even extending into Europe. It is the only country in the world that spans two continents, with territory in what is now Thrace, or Bulgaria, and reaching as far east as Persia, Syria, and Iraq. North of Turkey is the Black Sea, west the Aegean, and south the Mediterranean. Istanbul lies literally in both Europe and Asia Minor, spanning the Bosporus at the mouth of the Black Sea. Western Turkey, specifically the coastal region, was at various times occupied by the ancient Greeks, Romans, and Byzantines, who maintained their capital at Constantinople for centuries. Their strength enabled them to remain supreme in Constantinople for two centuries after the Ottomans had subjugated the rest of Turkey; the Byzantines were surrounded but not subdued.

Athens is only about 250 miles from Turkey across the Aegean. Although the thought is commonly expressed that Turkey is a bridge between Asia and Europe, it is closer to the truth to say that Turkey is a bridge between Asia and Greece, and its rugs reflect this heritage. This is particularly true of village looms. While cottage and nomadic weaving was never as prolific in Turkey as in Persia because of Turkey's early emphasis on commercialization, there were many fine specimens from Bergama, Demirici, Ghiordes, Kirsehir, Konya, Ladik, and Melas. Even some of the names sound Greek.

The earliest Turkish rugs were found in the mosque in Konya and were judged to be from the twelfth and thirteenth centuries. Five fragments and three whole rugs were found. Konya, more than 200 miles east and 100 miles north of the Mediterranean, is on an ancient trade route linking Syria and Mesopotamia and Europe. Although Konya is farther inland than the area subdued and ruled for profit by the Greeks, their influence is evident in the rug designs. When Marco Polo arrived in

Various decorations

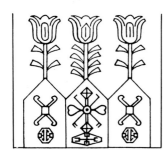

Ladik prayer rug tulips

Turkey in the thirteenth century he described the Greeks, Turks, and Armenians as living beside one another in idyllic harmony and making "the finest and most beautiful carpets in the world, and also silks . . ."

But there is evidence that highly evolved weaving existed many centuries before these early fragments. It is known from primitive drawings that the fat-tailed sheep and angora goat, both of which produce wool highly prized by weavers, have been cultivated since earliest times by Turkish herdsmen. More important, it has long been thought that pile weaving was developed by nomadic herders. Turkey is traversed by latitudinal mountains, and like Persia, much of the country is plateau land 3000 to 4000 feet above sea level. A nomadic population has existed there for centuries. The pattern of their lives has not changed through political upheaval and modernization, the rhythm of their movement depending instead on the seasons.

Interestingly, none of the indigenous tribes ever rose to the fore either numerically, culturally, or ideologically. By contrast, although Persia was defeated and occupied many times by foreigners, the vast majority of the population was Persian and by and large their own culture was assimilated by their conquerors rather than the reverse. This is not the case in Turkey, where the Turkic peoples, for whom the land was named, did not make their appearance until the sixth century A.D. Until then the country was politically and ethnically unstable. It could be said that Persia has always had a strong national consciousness, something that has come to Turkey only in the past 1000 years. It is interesting to speculate that the heritage of rug weaving grew concurrently with the assumption of a national identity, and certainly both have an unmistakable character.

The Hittites were actually the first people who settled in Anatolia and Mesopotamia, which they dominated from 1800 to 1400 B.C. During the following 2000 years the Persians, Greeks, and Armenians prevailed. Darius the Great went to Europe across the Bosporus by making a bridge of his galleys in the sixth century B.C. Later the land became a province of Rome. The word *anadolu* means "that which was conquered from the Byzantines."

The Armenians were a Balkan tribe that migrated to Asia Minor, chiefly the Caucasus, in 1200 B.C. According to Herodotus, they fought with Xerxes in the Graeco-Persian wars. Many of them fled the Caucasus and settled in a region in northwestern Persia. For centuries of changing boundaries this area, south of the Caucasus and between the Black and Caspian Seas, was a state known as Armenia. The Armenians have been characterized through the centuries by movement, partially because they adopted Christianity as the state religion in the third century, which of course was not understood by the Turks around them. They were invaded by the Turks, Babylonians, and Assyrians, yet their own culture flourished. They had a translation of the Bible by the fifth century, and they have taken rug weaving with them wherever they have migrated. During World War I the Turks deported numerous Armenians to Syria and Macedonia, fearing that they were joining the Russian army through the Caucasus. Understandably, rugs made in northeastern Turkey had certain similarities to Caucasian rugs, an affinity no doubt inspired not just by geographic proximity but also by the Armenian heritage. This is true even now, sixty years later.

It is thought that the name Turkey and its derivatives came from the Chinese name for a certain tribe, the T'ur Küe. In any case, the sixth century saw the first wave of Mongolian tribes moving west into Asia Minor, and these tribesmen did in fact become known as Turks. These nomadic people, forced out by the Chinese, had migrated as far as the Black Sea. Some traveled to the USSR and Sinkiang, the others to northwestern Iran, Asiatic Turkey, and Europe. At the end of the seventh century the latter group participated in the Arab conquest of Transoxiana and became part of Persia.

In 999 Bokhara and Samarkand came under Turkic rule. A similarity may be seen between the rugs from this region and the tribal rugs of Turkey. In each case a blunt approach to design and bold use of color are reminiscent of the other. Many of these Turks converted to the Islamic beliefs, and after the death of Mohammed they and the Arab Muslims conquered Turkey as part of Byzantium. Turkey became a Muslim state administered by the Turks and Persians, with the Islamic caliph as head of state.

These rulers were followed by the Seljuk Turks, another Oxus River tribe, and the Mongols. The great Ottoman Empire was founded by still another group of Turks, who were transplanted to Anatolia from the Oxus region by the Mongol invasions in the thirteenth century. They took power with diplomacy and gained acceptance among the reigning Seljuks by converting to the Muslim faith. They were superb administrators. It was not until 1453 that they took Constantinople, but from the thirteenth century on the general trend was toward their aggrandizement.

In effect, centuries of Turkish as well as Persian history were dominated by tribes that had originated in China and had migrated first to Transoxiana and then to richer southern territories. Ottoman domination was concurrent with the refinement and creation of a commercial market for Turkish rugs, at least as far as subsequent historians can determine. In 1377 the Osmanlis took the emirates of Ephesus and Tekke, the latter being the region of the rug-producing nomads. They held Bulgaria, part of Turkey from Ephesus to the Black Sea, and large portions of Asia Minor.

Even though it has had a foot in two continents for the past four centuries, Turkey has not been exposed to foreign influence in the same manner as Persia and the Caucasus. Of these three countries, Turkey has enjoyed the most stable society, and one result is that its rugs do not speak with the polyglot tongue of rugs from the more turbulent regions. During the past four centuries Turkey has not been subjugated by other nationalities or in any way forced to accept outside influence. The mixture of ideas so noticeable in Persian and Caucasian design is absent in Turkey. The Armenians and the Greeks have undoubtedly contributed to the Turkish rug, but since they have been there for so many centuries their ideas do not stand out as a foreign element.

Like every other rug-weaving area, the Turks began by weaving relatively small decorative rugs and (in their case) prayer rugs. They used the Ghiordes knot rather than the Persian Sehna knot. The Turkish knot may be said to have a collar, whereas the Persian knot is asymmetrical.

Partially because twentieth-century Turkish history has been so unstable, the enormous export production of the last century has been severely curtailed. Since World II Oushaks and Smyrnas have almost disappeared, and Sivas are rarely seen in the marketplace. There are of course many new factory rugs, but most of the modern designs are poor. Individuality has ceased almost entirely.

Borders

"Water" border (bicolored)

Latchhook border

Tulip and rosettes border

Carnation borders

Siebenbürger border

Prayer rug types

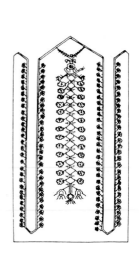

Kulah   Ghiordes

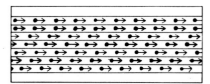

Prayer rug border

Detail of border

23. ANATOLIAN MAKRI

19th century, 5'2" × 3'7" [m. 1.60 × 1.10]
Warp: wool
Weft: wool, two shoots after each row of knots
Knotting: Ghiordes, wool, 48 knots per square inch
[770 per dm.²]

The term "Anatolian" applies to rugs woven in the towns of Kirsehir, Mudjur, Yuruk, and Makri as well as to a number of less easily identifiable tribal rugs. As a rule, these rugs are coarsely woven, but some of the older pieces are valued for their bold color and naive design.

Kirsehir prayer rugs are distinguished by their stepped niches. Mudjur rugs are squarish and also have stepped niches invariably on a red background. Yuruk is the coarsest in this group.

Makri is one of the southernmost weaving towns in Turkey, not far from the Mediterranean. This rug has a characteristic design, the rectangle being divided lengthwise into two or three sections, red and blue,

with pointed ends. Although it was made far from the Caucasus, it has some of the rough charm of those in Plates 54 and 64. It uses clean vegetable dyes (that is, the colors are clear and have not run). Like a Kazak, it has geometric figures in primary colors. Like Caucasian designs, it uses the outside star border, and the octagons in the left side of the field are rayed. On the sides of the inside border are carnations on stylized stems, and another version of the carnation on diagonal stems fills the red and blue fields.

Separating the red and blue fields is a ribbon border, and filling in the corner on the yellow ground are stylized triangles. Surprisingly, at the bottom is a diagonal band of angular *botehs,* the most common motif of Persian rugs. Above that is a narrow blue band of stylized cloudbands taken from the Chinese.

It is fascinating that a nineteenth-century rug from a little town in southern Turkey could have been influenced by designs from as far away as China and the Caucasus, but not surprising when one considers that the Mediterranean had already acted as a conduit for trade between East and West for five centuries.

26. GHIORDES

late 18th or early 19th century, 6'8" × 4'7" [m. 2.04 × 1.40]

Warp: wool
Weft: cotton, two shoots after each row of knots
Knotting: Ghiordes, wool, 108 knots per square inch [1730 per dm.²]

Ghiordes not only gave its name to the classic Turkish knot, but also to a tradition of splendid weavings. Influenced by the famous sixteenth-century Ottoman court production, the Ghiordes prayer rug remained unrivaled until the late nineteenth century. A lamp often hangs from the niche of the *mihrab* in a unichrome field with or without pillars, with a cartouche surmounting the *mihrab*. The border motif may be either seven stripes (representing the "seven skies of Allah") or floral motifs, often stylized in geometric patterns.

The area around Ghiordes has produced village rugs of larger format and coarser structure, identified by pleasant magentas and greens in a double-niche field. Among these is the Kis-Ghiordes (*kis* means "young girl"), which a maiden supposedly wove for her dowry. The background here is pale green and the floral borders predominantly pink, white, black, pale blue, and beige are also used to create an effect that is delicate but by no means weak.

The *mihrab* is decorated with flowers similar in shape to the hanging lamp in Plate 25. Cartouches at each end of the field and carnations on a slanted stem frame the interior. The seven small, symmetrical borders are characteristic of Ghiordes prayer rugs, as are the carnation borders. Another characteristic Ghiordes motif, a symbol of fertility, is two pomegranates growing from a serrated leaf or one hanging from the leaf.

One of the interesting features of the older prayer rugs is that they are marked by a slash across the back, caused by the extra stitches required to join the work of the several weavers customarily employed. For the sake of speed one child would work the middle section while two others wove the sides.

27. HEREKE

late 19th century, 6'6" × 4'10" [m. 2.00 × 1.50]
Warp: silk
Weft: silk
Knotting: Ghiordes, 200 knots per square inch [3100 per dm.²]

Hereke is on the outskirts of Istanbul and, in contrast to Oushak, claims no special tradition in the field of rug weaving. Its fame was derived entirely from an imperial court manufacture founded there in 1844 and closed at the end of the century.

Its production was limited to rugs of great fineness in knotting, which was the major yardstick for value at that time, and for a taste that had not extended beyond the boundaries of Europe. Very short pile and rich, red, open fields are characteristic of these rugs. Not being bound by a tradition, the design was sometimes derived from French Savonnerie sources but more often imitated complicated Persian models.

Preferred sizes were large. A peculiarity of the Herekes was a signature or initials on one of the outer borders near the fringe.

This example, a silk prayer rug, has a red interior field and wide brown borders with muted decoration in many tones of beige, off-white, brown, green, red, and pink.

The Arabic script indicates that the rug was made for a friend and follows with a passage from the Koran, but its main purpose was probably decorative.

It is interesting to compare the flowing lines of the *mihrab* with the structure in other Turkish prayer rugs, such as those in Plates 25, 26, 28, 29, and 30.

28. KULA PRAYER RUG

18th century, 6'1" × 4' [m. 1.85 × 1.22]
Warp: wool
Weft: wool, two to three shoots after each row of knots
Knotting: Ghiordes, wool, 112 knots per square inch
  [1800 per dm.²]

Kula is located about 100 miles east of Izmir and 50 miles southeast of Ghiordes. Together with Ghiordes and Ladik, it has traditionally produced the finest prayer rugs in Turkey.

Kulas differ from Ghiordes (Plate 26) by a more rectangular format, slightly coarser knotting, higher pile, and softer wool. The color range is usually lighter, with an abundance of yellows and deep reds.

While Kulas have many design elements in common with Ghiordes, they also have two unique field patterns. The first is a "tree of life" motif in a narrow field surmounted by a lampless *mihrab*. The second is a stylization of small houses, which were once interpreted as tombs and have earned this rug type the name "cemetery Kula."

It is interesting to note that this *mihrab* is held up by two columns and that there are six borders with small, distinctive flowers rather than the seven typical of a Ghiordes rug. The outside border is somewhat similar to the inside border in Plate 23, probably a derivative of the Chinese cloudband.

Although the rug is antique, the colors are as modern as one could wish today.

29. LADIK PRAYER RUG

18th century, 5′4″ × 3′10″ [m. 1.63 × 1.09]
Warp: wool
Weft: wool, two shoots after each row of knots
Knotting: Ghiordes, wool, 117 knots per square inch
   [1880 per dm.²]

These most cherished of all Turkish rugs, distinguished by the long-stemmed horizontal tulips over the *mihrab*, come from Ladik (now called Yorganladik), a city in south-central Turkey that produced them for over four centuries. The knotting in a Ladik is very fine by Turkish standards, and the color scheme is almost always red and blue against a light background.

There are two characteristic Ladik designs. In the older one there are six pillars in the field in the order one-two-two-one, a pattern that is unrealistic from an architectural standpoint but graceful from an aesthetic standpoint. The other type, shown here, has up to three subsidiary niches in the lower section of the field and tulips over the topmost *mihrab*.

Ladik rugs range from the most elegant to the most primitive and energetic. This one is an irregular size, as if woven on a nomad's loom, and is focused by the brilliant red and blue areas in its field. The central arch of the *mihrab* is offset by two lower arches over which are two distinct fields of decoration, as was the style in the eighteenth century. In the blue area are serrated leaves, stars, and carnations; above that, a carnation-and-vine border; and above that, extravagantly hooked mud-colored triangles. Over that is another red area decorated by the very striking tulips.

The wide central border is decorated with a simple iris-and-snowflake design. With the other borders, almost all of which are on a pale background, it contrasts pleasantly with the brightly colored field.

Like the rug in Plate 23, this is original art: The dye is clean, the packing fine, and the definition sharp, but here the weave is fine rather than coarse. It does not conform to modern aesthetic rules, but the various parts—the blue slice, white borders, and red sections—combine to effect a harmonious, if elusive, whole.

30. MELAS

early 19th century, 4′10″ × 3′10″ [m. 1.50 × 1.18]
Warp: wool
Weft: wool, three shoots after each row of knots
Knotting: Ghiordes, wool, 49 knots per square inch
   [780 per dm.²]

Melas is a province in southwestern Turkey on the Aegean Sea, and the rugs from that area are as primitive as the land, with the vigor of an ocean breeze. They are small—never larger than six by four feet—and usually include some red. Their design is strong and asymmetrical. The niche in a prayer rug is often in the odd shape of an indented lozenge, and in modern production the characteristic red has become brown.

In a sense a rug from Melas is like a Volkswagen—sturdy, modest, and happy. Here the inside of the *mihrab* is decorated with carnations at a slant, as well as with irregular diamonds and triangles. The wide border is unusual, filled with odd polygons, rosettes on bifurcated stems, and arrows, a Chinese derivative. The inside border is an odd barber stripe, the outside a battlement stripe. The niche is red, a color that is picked up in much of the incidental decoration. The widest border has a light brown background, and the other colors include white, pale green, a bit of purple, and black tracery.

Rugs from Melas are as a rule coarsely knotted. An effect is produced that is at once irregular and, since the details are all big, vital. In this rug even the weft and warp are red, and traces of it may be seen through the tufts.

31. OUSHAK

19th century, 13′ × 9′11″ [m. 3.95 × 3.00]
Warp: cotton
Weft: cotton, two shoots after each row of knots
Knotting: Ghiordes, wool, 48 knots per square inch
  [770 per dm.²]

The village of Oushak in central Turkey has produced rugs of great beauty ever since the sixteenth century; the rugs immortalized by painters are almost always Oushaks. [A "Lotto" is an Oushak like the one in "The Alms of S. Anthony" (1542); "Holbein" is an Oushak like the one in "The Ambassadors," by Hans Holbein the Younger.] Oushaks were among the first Oriental rugs exported to America, and their designs were copied by the English Axminster factories as early as the eighteenth century.

It is clear that the reason for the Oushaks' success in an alien culture is that they are among the most pleasing of all Oriental rugs to the Western eye. Their fire red warms a room on a cold day in Boston, Milan, or York.

The medallions are regular and in classic proportions. More primitive styles have given way to sophistication of color and form. An early Oushak is a timeless piece of art, as appropriate today as it was when Gilbert Stuart painted George Washington standing on one.

The older Oushaks were usually dark red and blue, with medallions and arabesques close to the Persian style, but the most famous ones had a red background with a strong yellow in the designs. Later Oushaks became known for the beauty of their pastels; an example is this nineteenth-century carpet, where the background is rose, the borders and vases blue and green. The medallions are vases or stylized tulips filled in with a version of the crab design and separated by the Tibetan *vajra* (the little cross inside a diamond outline). The tulip is an early eighteenth-century design.

This is a large carpet. It is interesting to compare it with rugs in Plates 42, 44, and 55. Although it was meant to dignify an entrance or fill an odd hallway, the carpet has given weavers a challenge that has produced a number of striking designs.

32. KILIM ANATOL

early 20th century, 12'6" × 5'5" [m. 3.80 × 1.64]
Warp: wool
Knotting: flat weave, pile wool

Because pile carpets were so highly prized, flat weaves were not made for the Western market until very recently. Thus, a higher percentage of antique Kilims were made for family use. (*Kilim* is the general term for flat-weave Oriental rugs.) Like this one, they are highly irregular, probably woven on a nomad's loom.

Because the designs are woven by a continuous thread passing diagonally through the weft and warp threads rather than many individual knots, Kilim designs consist of angles and straight lines. It is impossible to put a curved line on what is essentially the structure of graph paper. Because of this structure, the weaving is divided between colors, resulting in slits.

Although this runner has the three field medallions typical of the Caucasus and many Kilims were produced in that area, their medallions are usually more decorated than this, appearing as octagons and even more complex shapes. The unbroken diagonal shapes here are characteristic of Anatolian Kilims.

It is interesting to note that the border of this rug is the carnation or rosette with leaf border done in the Kilim stitch, which renders it completely different in appearance from, for example, that in Plate 26, where it appears to be geometric, or that in Plate 1, where it is not geometric but has more space. The top figure has a white background and the two bottom figures a red one. Green and beige are also used. The background is a striking indigo blue, picked up in other details of the border and medallions.

At the upper left corner of the field are two animals facing each other, and on the right is a date or signature.

33. YURUK

early 20th century, 4′10″ × 3′4″ [m. 1.50 × 1.00]
Warp: wool
Weft: wool
Knotting: Ghiordes, 100 knots per square inch [1550 per dm.²]

These nomadic rugs are made by a Kurdish mountain tribe nearer to the Persian border than to the coast with its Greek influence. But a surprising similarity to Caucasian design is their dominant visual character. The use of the latchhook, a striking central figure (here, a diamond), and scattered background embellishments would all indicate a kinship to that region.

As a rule, these products have a rather long pile and use earthy brown and reds, blue, black, and white, as here. This example, which employs an unusual amount of white, has a rare aura of sophistication.

THE CAUCASUS

THE CAUCASUS IS DESCRIBED by Leo Tolstoy in these words:

The morning was crystal clear. Suddenly he saw, at what seemed to him at first glance to be about twenty paces away, gigantic pure white masses with gentle curves and fantastical airy summits minutely outlined against the distant sky. When he realized the distance between himself and them and the sky, and the whole immensity of those mountains, and their infinite beauty, he feared lest it prove to be a mirage or a dream. . . .[1]

The Caucasus is not only a fierce and beautiful mountain range between the Black and Caspian Seas but also a way of life. Although it has been known for centuries as the only overland path between Europe and Asia, the terrain is so wild, so remote, and so poor that it has never been even a minor trade route. Instead, it became a refuge for outlawed, rebellious, and idiosyncratic tribes, some of whom are so entrenched in the mountains that they can be reached only at certain times of the year. It is impossible to define the Caucasus in terms of political boundaries because those boundaries have changed so often through the years. The mountains stretch for 400 miles and are among the most stunning and hostile in the world. There are 900 glaciers and 12 peaks higher than the highest Alp in the 125 miles between Mt. Kazbek and Mt. Elbruz. Mt. Elbruz, the highest, is so high that in Greek legend Zeus chained Prometheus there, 18,493 feet above the sea, to punish him for bringing fire to man. From a geological point of view the formation is interestingly simple, as it has only one ridge that stretches its entire length and is no wider than 120 miles at its highest point. To the south the mountains are protected by a smaller range in Georgia, known as the Little Caucasus, that runs almost parallel to them.

1. Tolstoy, Leo, *The Cossacks*, trans. Rosemary Edmonds, Penguin Books, Harmondsworth, Middlesex, England, 1960.

Animal and human figures

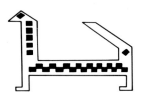

Dogs

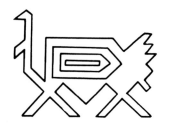

Camels

Tolstoy was not the only Russian writer who lived in the Caucasus during his military service and later wrote about it. The best known of the other writers is Lermontov. Like Tolstoy, he came to respect the strong individuality of his Caucasian opponents. The personality of the land itself as well as its people inspired these writers. Such a distinct sense of place and populace produced the strong geometric figures that make Caucasian rugs, particularly the Kazaks, among the most readily identifiable of Oriental rugs. A disproportionate number of Caucasian rugs is included in this selection because they are the most popular Oriental rugs on the market today. Their small size, brilliant coloring, and lustrous wool give them a gemlike quality that a larger rug could never possess. Their coloring and design make them ideally suited to modern interiors. Their vivid personality has influenced some of the greatest Slavic artists, like Kandinsky, and, in turn, the School of Paris artists of the Thirties.

Northwest of Persia and northeast of Turkey, the Caucasus is the real heart of the rug world. Even though it was rarely used as a trade route between East and West, it is so central that its art was influenced by all the important rug traditions from Turkey to China. Baku, for instance, is only 100 miles from Tabriz, as is Tiflis. When Marco Polo traveled to China and the court of Kubla Khan in the fourteenth century he went through Georgia, Armenia, Kurdistan, and Ispahan, and on the way back he entered the Caucasus after having traveled overland from the distant Indian Ocean.

Caucasian rugs are not just a cross between the floral delicacy of Persian rugs and the geometric stylization of Turkish rugs. They are original designs, often stamped with the personality of the weaver and even signed. There are actually more signed rugs from the Caucasus than from any other area. Although simple hard-edge abstractions are a common stage in the development of the art of nomadic or semi-nomadic tribes, such as the American Indians, Scythians, or Greeks, the vibrance and complexity of these rugs reflect the richness of life in one of the most magnificent places in the world. They are beyond classification and beyond simplicity.

The mark of the maker, called by anthropologists a naive sort of narcissism, is enjoyed by many present-day artists. One quality of primitive art more difficult for us to understand in the twentieth century is a background of hardship. As late as 1840 Lermontov wrote, in *A Hero of Our Time,*

The hut was built with one wall against a cliff; three slippery wet steps led to its door. I groped my way in and ran smack into a cow (with these people a cattle shed replaces a vestibule). I did not know which way to turn: here, sheep were bleating, there, a dog was growling. Fortunately, a dim light gleamed on one side and helped me to find another opening in the guise of a doorway. There, a rather entertaining picture was disclosed. The spacious hut, whose roof rested on two smoke-blackened posts, was full of people. In the center, there crackled a small fire built on the ground, and the smoke, forced back by the wind from the hole in the roof, spread all around in such a thick pall that, for a long time, I could not see around me: by the fire sat two old women, a multitude of children, and one lean Georgian, all of them in rags.[2]

But the people of the Caucasus have understood the forms of other cultures and managed to mold them into a brilliant style of their own. After all, it is a part of the world that has no indigenous heritage like China or Persia. It is as if an artist saw the original forms through a rather sophisticated prism that changed them all in the same way, but in fact the weaver who portrayed them was an illiterate herder on a snow-covered mountain in Asia in a barely lit sod house half dug in the ground or a tent filled with smoke. It is astonishing that what came from such a loom was fresh. The Islamic arabesque was stepped; that is, the curves were described as a series of right angles. The medallion, vase types, and palmetto of Persia were similarly treated in a geometric manner. From Anatolia came the Shirvan border, the crab, and the warmth. The rigidity of Turkestan was occasionally used for emphasis, but never merely out of custom. The Chinese dragon, swastika, and borders were derived and transformed. The color of Samarkand and the sensuality of India were melded into the weft and warp. And in the end, although the Caucasian style is derivative, it stands on its own merits as a unique regional style. The Caucasians' sense of humor is seen in the tiny figures in a relatively huge geometric landscape, the little household animals, and the simple, funny, Grandma Moses-like detail. It is an incongruity of wit rather than a didactic contrast stemming from the Islamic fear of God. More powerful in its own way is the Kazak sunburst, or eagle, in all its versions.

Bird

The rugs that come from the Caucasus are much more important than their small size would warrant. They include Sumarks, Karabaghs, Gendjes, Vernés, Shirvans, Chilas, Chichis, Lesghis, Daghestans, and Bakus, besides the well-known Kazaks. It is thought that some of the rugs depicted by the Italian painters of the thirteenth and fourteenth centuries were Caucasian.

Akstafa peacock

In Turkish, *kazak* means "free man," which reflects the attitude the rest of the world has always had toward the tribes of the Caucasus. Pliny the Elder wrote that when the Romans traveled through the Caucasus to settle on the coast of the Black Sea they took eighty interpreters with them to translate for the multitude of peoples that lived there. In the seventh century the Scyths (noted for their weaving expertise, as seen in Pasyrik rug), Kurds, Georgians, and Armenians surged through the Caucasus, and Turkish tribes invaded and settled there from the eleventh to the fourteenth centuries. In Daghestan, a region 300 miles long west of the Caspian Sea, are found the ruins of an 18- to 20-foot wall between Derbent and Koushan studded with 43 castles. Perhaps it was built as protection against Alexander the Great, who never took the Caucasus, or against Tamerlane and the Golden Horde. There is only one opening in the wall.

Man and woman

2. Lermontov, Mikhail, *A Hero of Our Time*, trans. Vladimir Nabokov with Dmitri Nabokov, Doubleday, Anchor Books, Garden City, N.Y., 1958.

Verneh, similar to Gendje

Gendje

Lesghi

Kuba version of Lesghi

Politically, the Caucasus was part of Persia through the Middle Ages. In 1722 the Slavs began to prize the mountains away from the Ottoman Empire, and by 1785 they had absorbed the North Caucasus. In 1864 Russia announced that it had finally conquered the entire region: For 142 years the Russians had been fighting to subdue the fiercely independent natives of the Caucasus.

The tribes always lived together under the common laws naturally imposed by small territorial boundaries, but each tribe had individual customs. As the majority were nomadic tribes, the little territory they claimed shifted from season to season. The earth was poor and the sheep as tough and scrawny as their masters. They owed nothing to anyone and bore themselves proudly, even those that never traveled farther than one mountain away from their *kosh* (stone house in the ground). Their characteristic coat, called a *burka,* was a wide-shouldered cape made of goat hair so thick it repelled the rain and snow. Under this they wore a tunic and caftan over a full blouse, loose-ankled boots, and a great fur hat. In their belts they stuck the *kindjal,* a pretty two-fluted dagger, gay but mortal. This colorful costume·was also sensible. When the weather changed, a mountaineer could just add or peel off a layer of clothing.

Some of the better-known tribes in the Caucasus were the Circassians, the Cossacks, the Norsemen, a group of Wurttemburg Germans, the Tartars, the Buddhist Kalmucks, the Ingush, the Balkans, and the Karachays. The weavers among them were Chechen, Lesghi, Circassians, and Armenians and Persians.

The Circassians, who occupied all the northwestern stretch and held out longest against the Russians, were noted for their horses and women, which they frequently sold to other people. The men became Turkish Janissaries and members of the Mameluke Corps of Egypt, and the women bred their distinctive good looks into all the great families of Turkey. They were tall and dark, with aristocratic faces and striking eyes. The word *Caucasus* is thought to be a corruption of their name.

Not surprisingly, the spirited Caucasian tribes had at best an uneasy truce with the Russians. Because the area was so far from any Russian outpost, officers were posted there as punishment and cadets were sent there to serve time before their first big promotion. Occasionally it was chosen as a place of personal exile to save money, for, as Tolstoy commented, the only thing for a soldier to do there was drink, hunt, and fall in love. Presumably none of those activities was very expensive in 1851. Tolstoy wrote about his artillery regiment in a story called *The Cossacks.* His hero, young Olenin, travels to the Caucasus for the first time dreaming of the wild Circassian girl he will tame, educate, and conquer society with when he returns. He is billeted with a tribe of Russian Cossacks who settled there several generations before with the Chechen (who have, incidentally, woven some of the most beautiful rugs of the whole region). The Cossacks maintain an unreliable peace with the Tartars across the river, both being menaced by the Abreks, or hostile Circassians, who live beyond the Tartars. Tolstoy describes the nuances of the relationship between the Russian guard and the Cossacks as follows:

Dwelling among the Chechens, the Cossacks intermarried with them and adopted the manners and customs of the hill tribes, though they still retained the Russian language and the Old Faith in all its purity. According to a tradition still existing Tsar Ivan the Terrible came to the Terek River, sent for the Cossack elders and gave them the land on this side of the river, exhorting them to remain friendly to Russia and promising not to enforce his rule upon them nor oblige them to change their faith. Ever since, the Cossacks have claimed relationship with the Chechens, and love of freedom, of leisure, plunder and war have been their most notable traits. Russian influence shows itself only in a detrimental way, by interference at elections, the confiscation of church-bells and the presence of troops who are quartered in the country, or march through it. A Cossack is less inclined to hate the Chechen brave, the *dzhigit*, who may well have killed his brother, than the Russian soldier billeted on him for the defense of his village but who has fouled his cottage by smoking in it. He respects his enemy the hillsman, but despises the soldier, who is in his eyes an alien and an oppressor. In fact, the Cossack regards the Russian peasant as a foreign, outlandish, despicable creature, of whom he sees specimens enough in the hawkers and Ukrainian immigrants whom he contemptuously calls "wool-combers." For the Cossack, to be smartly dressed means to be dressed like a Circassian. The best weapons are obtained from the hillsmen, and the best horses are bought or stolen from them. The young Cossack brave prides himself on his knowledge of the Tartar language, and when carousing talks Tartar even to his fellow Cossack. In spite of all this, this small Christian clan, stranded in a tiny corner of the earth, surrounded by half-savage Mohammedan tribes and Russian soldiers, considers itself highly advanced, acknowledges none but Cossacks as human beings and despises everybody else. . . .[3]

It is interesting to note that in the story there are Cossack fortresses and Russian fortresses, there is the Nogay tribe that lives on the steppe behind the Cossacks, and there are the Tartars. They all believe that the real enemy, the only one worth fighting, is the Abreks, yet each group feels a measure of hostility toward the others. Of course, Olenin falls in love with a beautiful Circassian-Cossack girl, to whom he offers marriage and with it the rich life of a Russian noble. She returns his affection until one of her fellow Cossacks is wounded fighting the Abreks, and then she turns on Olenin. Tolstoy used the frustration of the romance to focus his observations and ideas, and in the end he wrote about a question of blood, as serious as the mountains.

There are no real cities in the Caucasus. Shemakh, on the east coast of the Black Sea, was a major rug-weaving center. Baku, a modern oil town on the coast of the Caspian Sea, is populated by Armenians and Tartars, Christian and Mohammedan. An old Persian city settled by Zoroaster and the Parsees of Bombay, its sea view is now dominated by the huge insect outlines of oil derricks and rigs. Then there is Tiflis, the capital of Georgia, where Stalin grew up, an old Asiatic center until the war. Since then it has become an important industrial and economic force. The

Kazak, similar to Turkestan

Eagle Kazak

Kazak (background)

3. Tolstoy, Leo, *The Cossacks*, trans. Rosemary Edmonds, Penguin Books, Harmondsworth, Middlesex, England, 1960.

Kazak Borjalu spider

Shirvan star

Kazak "S"

Anchor

Scorpion

Black Sea area, while heavily populated in relation to the rest of the region, is noted for its warm summer resorts for the Soviet Union, not its cosmopolitan life. In any case, more popular resorts, including the Crimean and Odessa, are on the west coast.

After the revolution in 1917, the Caucasus split away from Russia to form three independent states: Georgia, Armenia, and Azerbaidzhan, which became republics of the USSR in 1936. As a political hideout and a natural home for adventurers, the Caucasus was always the Wild West of Russia. Stalin, a native, knew its potential as an underground refuge for dissenters, and during World War II he had many of the tribes relocated. In keeping with the Soviet policy of repression of the individual, he knew it was necessary to exercise absolute control over people of such strong character. In 1943 the Chechen, Ingush, Balkar, and Karachay tribes were deported to Siberia (Paraguay offered the Kalmucks sanctuary). The gradual return of these tribes to the Caucasus has been reported over time.

All of these factors—the territorial character, the nomadic life of poverty, and the fierce personality of the tribes—have contributed to the look and design of the rugs. With the exception of a few early-nineteenth-century Karabaghs influenced by French Savonnerie decoration, the rugs invariably have a severe design, more often geometric than not. Then colors, even in the paler rugs, are bold. Only natural dyes were used, even after the introduction of aniline dyes, from 1870 to 1920. Wool was taken from mountain sheep and gleams with a particular luster, white being used almost invariably for the warp and colors for the weft. The Ghiordes knot was adopted throughout the Caucasus. As most of the weavers were seminomadic, the rugs were woven on small portable looms that limited the design to four by six feet or a narrow runner up to six feet long. The only exceptions are room-sized flat-woven Soumaks. Oddly enough, the length of the pile is thicker in the south and diminishes in the north. The rugs from the Talish, Moghan, Kazak, Armenian, and Karabagh districts are thicker and coarser than those from the Shirvan, Georgian, Lesghistan, and Daghestan regions.

Basically, the rugs of the Caucasus are tribal. What may be named a Baku actually comes from a tribe that markets its rugs to that city as the closest outlet for its wares. Soumak rugs, though named for the city Shamakh, are made by tribes dwelling in several districts. This practice of nomenclature was used in Turkey as well.

Until World War I, Caucasian rugs were rarely woven for export, and they are considered original and authentic in all respects. Subsequent to the Russian Revolution of 1917, Caucasian rug weaving dropped to an all-time low, so a Caucasian from the period between the two wars is rare. The Russian and Pakistani copies that have been made since 1960 are too new looking and ordinary to be worth mention. The great rug-weaving days of the Caucasus are over, just as they are in most of the rest of the world. The label "Cabistan," also spelled Cabristan or Kabistan, actually means nothing. At one time it was incorrectly used to identify almost half of all Caucasian production. The term *Kuba* refers to a district in the northeast Caucasus on the shores of the Caspian Sea that included a number of weaving villages. As mentioned previously Caucasian rugs are dated more frequently than rugs from other areas. It has been theorized that the Armenians, who handed them down through their families, did this as a matter of record and that other groups emulated their custom.

This classification of Caucasian rugs will follow, with few exceptions, the lines set by the distinguished scholar Ulrich Schurmann. Most of the rugs pictured, though dating from the nineteenth and early twentieth centuries, are in a good state of preservation.

In part, it is extraordinary to consider that rugs of such verve and color come from a barren, poor life. Causasian life is subject to strong geographic, religious, and cultural influences. But the strongest influence was the one that has perhaps contributed more to all of the arts than any other: solitude.

Cross

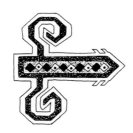

Sword, Perepedil

Ram's horns, Perepedil (usurma)

Flowers

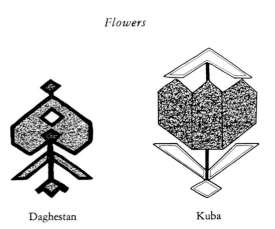

Daghestan   Kuba

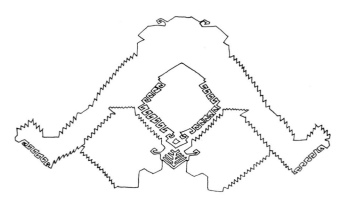

Soumak dragon motif, overall design

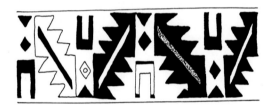

Two less well-defined versions
of the running-dog

Wineglass and leaf

Shirvan, carnation, similar to
Turkish carnation

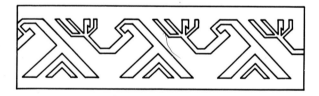

Shirvan, antique

Shirvan, stepped

Kuba, Georgian, or running
dog, usually in pink and dark
blue

Shirvan, stepped (variant)

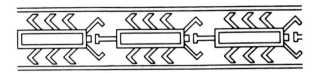

Scorpion

Kazak

Chichi characteristic. The diagonal bar in the design is often red and white, hence the sobriquet "barber pole border."

Flowers

Crenellated edge

34. DAGHESTAN

late 19th century, 4′11″ × 3′6″ [m. 1.52 × 1.09]
Warp: wool
Weft: wool, two shoots after each row of knots
Knotting: Ghiordes, wool, 17 knots per square inch
[1870 per dm.²]

Daghestan, an area north of Kuba, produces rugs of a construction unique in the Caucasus. The warp threads, which in other rugs are almost invariably horizontal, are on a diagonal that is sometimes as pronounced as 75 degrees. They are tightly woven, and the result is strong and supple. Another anomaly of the Daghestan region is the fact that even though it is in the northern part of the Caucasus the pile of its rugs is as thick as that of Kazaks or Karabaghs.

A honeycombed white field decorated with a variety of multicolored flowers is a classic Daghestan type. The wide red border contains a remnant of a dragon's head, and the edges are bound in red and white.

The Gothic arch indicates a fairly early date. It symbolizes a clean, honest walk into a mosque, unlike some of the diminished later arches that are almost indentations in the line of the *mihrab* rather than an architectural feature.

The rug is dated twice, once on either side of the arch, with the date 1311 *Hegira*, which is equivalent to 1893. Even though rugs were occasionally backdated to make them appear to be antiques, this date is acknowledged to be original.

A little comb, one of the weaver's tools, has been woven into the inside of the arch.

Since these are such small, gay rugs, they are particularly attractive as wall hangings.

35. DAGHESTAN

1841/2, 4′9″ × 3′8″ [m. 1.46 × 1.14]
Warp: wool
Weft: wool, two shoots after each row of knots
Knotting: Ghiordes, wool, 154 knots per square inch
 [2450 per dm.²]

This rug is a collector's fantasy, for it tells a story. In the center is a picture of a hunter on horseback holding the points of a stag being brought down by a dog. The hunter crouches over the horse at such an odd angle that he may be dead or wounded. In the background are trees and a red sky.

Over this scene is a Persian inscription about the hunt. It begins by saying that the rug was ordered by Hussein from another town "in memory of my father." (Persian writing is read from right to left.) Because of the stylization in weaving, an inscription is difficult to read unless it is quite familiar. While Hussein, a name as common as George in Persia, is easy to read, his last name is impossible, and most of the message is lost. As a result, the inscription has been described as a "poem without balance."

The portrait of Hussein, presumably, is below the picture of the hunt. He is a bearded young man wearing earrings, with a dolorous face.

The rug is dated in the outside corner of the inscription on the left. It reads 1257 in Islamic script, which means it was woven in 1841. Although it is dated in Muslim numerals, the rug shows a face, which was outside the Islamic code of ethics. The weaver must have been a Muslim and Hussein a nonbeliever. Such is the power of the patron.

Typical of Daghestan products is the white background. It is interesting to note that the white is balanced by red, and the red flower stalks on either side of Hussein's face are quite beautiful. The rug is composed of simply decorated, substantial blocks of color, unlike most highly patterned Caucasian rugs.

36. DAGHESTAN

19th century, 4'7" × 3'3" [m 1.38 × 0.98]
Warp: wool
Weft: wool, two shoots after each row of knots
Knotting: Ghiordes, wool, 135 knots per square inch
    [2150 per dm.²]

Like the rug in Plate 34, this is a characteristic Daghestan. Although the ground is darker and it is not a prayer rug, the design is essentially the same. The characteristic white background filled with a variety of multicolored flowers could be seen as a design on the diagonal, following the warp threads. The borders are a crenellated edge, flowers in a row, and the vestigial dragon, but in this example they play a more prominent part than in Plate 34.

37. DAGHESTAN

mid-19th century, 7'2" × 3'7" [m. 2.23 × 1.12]
Warp: wool
Weft: wool, two shoots after each row of knots
Knotting: Ghiordes, wool, 130 knots per square inch
  [2100 per dm.²]

One of the most popular designs in history has been stripes, plain, gaudy, quiet, or vibrant. Designed to accommodate any environment, they have been used on cloth from French muslin to the most opulent of brocades.

Characteristic of the Islamic region, these stripes are not regular. The basic pattern is black, yellow, blue, white, red, white, but this sequence is varied three times in the top half of the rug to include pink and green. The stripes are decorated with bicolored squares at intervals alternating with the ones on the next stripe. The strength of the rug lies in the bright show of many colors displayed in a controlled manner.

The main border is a variation of the dragon border in Plates 34 and 36, and the other two borders are a very simplified version of the vine and leaf.

This piece is a fascinating design. Other areas of the Caucasus that use stripes are the Karabagh district, where the Schuscha tribe decorates them with *botehs*; the Gendje; the Shirvan, where they are sometimes used in prayer rugs, and the Baku, where they are indicated by *botehs* alone (see Plate 40). In all of these cases the stripes are on the diagonal, used as a counterpoint against the vertical and horizontal borders. There are also stripes that run parallel to the borders from the Baku and Kuba regions and on runners from the Karabagh (see Plate 43).

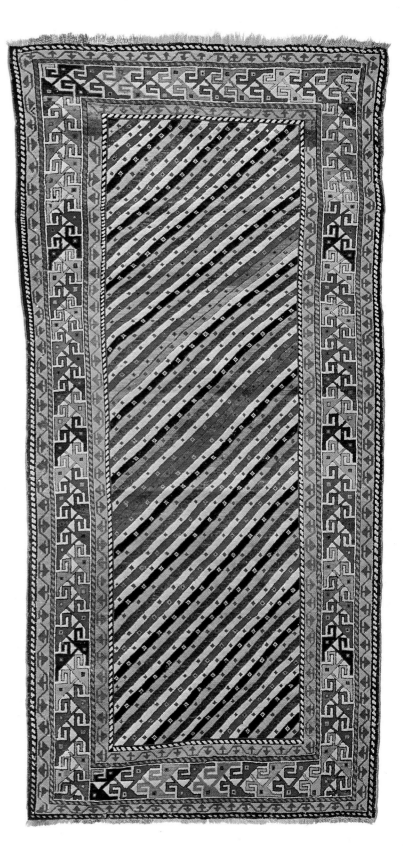

38. DERBENT

late 19th century, 5'1" × 4'3" [m. 1.58 × 1.32]
Warp: wool
Weft: wool, two shoots after each row of knots
Knotting: Ghiordes, wool, 108 knots per square inch
[1674 per dm.²]

39. DERBENT

19th century, 5'2" × 3'6" [m. 1.60 × 1.08]
Warp: wool
Weft: wool, two shoots after each row of knots
Knotting: Ghiordes, wool, 90 knots per square inch
[1700 per dm.²]

Derbent is a city on the Caspian Sea just north of the Great Caucasian Range. Except for very old pieces, its rugs have no particular style of their own but have borrowed from the more distinctive designs of other areas. The weft and warp frequently have cotton mixed into the wool, and in most cases the technique is thought to be casual. Often the dark colors predominate.

These two pieces are a happy exception to the preceding remarks. They are both knotted finely enough to give them strength, and since they are woven on light grounds they do not have the somber quality one associates with Derbent carpets. They do have a certain similarity to the Daghestans in Plates 34 and 36, more in feeling than in literal detail. The colors are beige, white, blue, pink, yellow, and green.

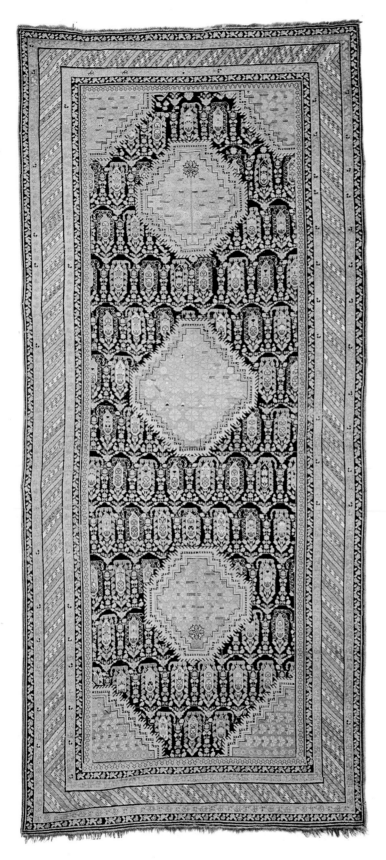

40. BAKU CHILA

ca. 1800, 12'5" × 5'2" [m. 3.75 × 1.60]
Warp: wool
Weft: wool, two shoots after each row of knots
Knotting: Ghiordes, wool, 100 knots per square inch
  [1600 per dm.²]

Baku is the only town of any size in the Caucasus. Owing to the discovery of oil in the area, it has grown quite a lot in this century. The rugs of Baku, like those made throughout the Caucasus, are noted for the use of certain characteristic motifs and techniques that not only identify them for what they are but also make it easier to know how good one is. Differences between rugs are due to the weaver's style, taste, and imagination.

In Baku, the stable elements are design, color, and technique. The *boteh* motif is used extensively, in every form and as a single or group decoration. The colors are, oddly enough, blue and brown (compare Plates 97 and 98). Here the blue is almost invariably pale, although sometimes a bright turquoise, and the brown typically pale but occasionally in other shades. The background is dark blue or black. Often one of the borders is composed of diagonal stripes in the shades used in the rug.

This particular rug is probably from Chila, a nearby village whose rugs were classified as Baku because they were exported through that city. The medallions in a rug made in Baku proper are laid end to end, and in this example they are not touching, which is typical of Chila. The flowers in the medallions are characteristic of a Samarkand or a Persian garden rug in their shape and regularity and in the structure of the vines.

The *botehs* in this rug are almost straight up, rather than hooked or birdlike, crowding the background with "clusters of leaves." The background is black, the colors blue and brown, and the border made of diagonal stripes in the colors of the field. The inside border, called a crenellated edge because it resembles battlements, is used throughout the Caucasus.

41. GENDJE

19th century, 9'5" × 4'6" [m. 2.93 × 1.40]
Warp: wool
Weft: wool, on shoot after each row of knots
Knotting: Ghiordes, wool, 77 knots per square inch
[1200 per dm.²]

This is a fairly rare dragon rug. Although it has the appearance of flat-woven Soumak, it is from the Gendje region. Apart from its striking and unusual design, this rug is a good example of the Caucasian stylization of forms from elsewhere: Almost everything in it is a popular design from another region. Included are the dragon motif, *botehs*, flowers, rosettes, swastikas, birds, animals, cloudbands, and crabs from Persia, Turkey, and China, all depicted with Caucasian punch. The colors are a spectrum of reds, yellow, blue, green, orange, and white on a dark blue background.

Gendje is bordered by the Kazak, Karabagh, and Shirvan areas. The structure of its rugs is similar to that of the Kazaks in terms of pile, warp, and weft, but this one does not have the Kazaks' characteristic coarseness. Gendjes show more variety of technique than Kazaks.

It is interesting to compare this rug with others in this book. Even the simple vine-and-flower border seen in Plate 44 or 47 has been transformed by hard edges into a totally different look. The field, which has the rhythm of an all-over design, is actually an irregular design that changes when it should repeat itself (compare Plate 78). Dragon rugs are often irregular, but because of the hard edges this one appears regular at first. It is similar to a Shirvan (see Plate 75), except for the hard edges, and to Kubas like those in Plates 48, 50, and 57.

This design is rather loose for its type. In the center of the field are a series of crabs in blue flowers outlined by paler dragon heads in green and yellow and cloudbands in white. The rest is like a jigsaw puzzle.

42. KARABAGH RUNNER

19th century, 12'9" × 3'10" [m. 3.95 × 1.20]
Warp: wool
Weft: wool, two shoots after each row of knots
Knotting: Ghiordes, wool, 64 knots per square inch
[1020 per dm.²]

This is the first of three Karabagh rugs. It is a marvelous example of delicate Persian designs angled and made geometric when woven by a Caucasian. It is easy to see the similarities between this particular rug and the classical all-over flower and tendril motifs in Plate 4 and in the ground outside the medallion in Plates 22, 7, and 13. The geometric design conveys a totally different feeling, less sensual, sharper, and, seen face up on a page with the simple flowers outlined in black, having a calico quality. Here the multicolored flowers are on a bright red ground.

This rug has only 64 knots per square inch, which is fairly coarse. The Karabagh district is in the south adjacent to the Kazak area, and the structure of its rugs is not unlike that of the Kazaks. They are coarsely woven, and often there are no fringes but a *kilim* at the end of the rug. The warp is bound in red or another color, and the three-ply warp and double weft are wool.

In the Karabagh black is used for emphasis, for example, as the background in the middle border of this rug. Actually, all three of these borders are unusual. The two narrow ones have almost an ideogrammatic quality, and the one in the center, while it is a variation of the leaf-and-vine border, is much stronger graphically than, for example, the one in Plate 38. The vine is accented by arrow-like leaves and small triangles of color in its interstices, and the flowers have the same heavy, bold quality.

Runners are not unusual in the Karabagh section of the Caucasus. Many of them are floral; some are not as angular as this one but even more Persian, like that in Plate 43; and some have medallions the length of the rug.

43. KARABAGH

mid-19th century, 19'8" × 3'9" [m. 6.10 × 1.17]
Warp: wool
Weft: wool, two shoots after each row of knots
Knotting: Ghiordes, wool, 80 knots per square inch
[1280 per dm.²]

This picture is one end of a nineteen-foot runner. It has the floral quality characteristic of the Karabagh organized in the form of stripes. One of the most popular types is the rectangular rug with multicolored *boteh* stripes similar to those of the Baku region (single-color *boteh* stripes from the Baku region are shown in Plate 40; Plate 37 shows another interpretation of stripes). The predominant colors are peach, red, brown, and white.

Although the knotting is coarse by Persian standards, the detail in this rug is particularly fine. There is very little irregularity in the border and almost none in the five stripes, which are identical motifs varying the colors.

Karabagh is at the southern end of the Caucasus, and nowhere do Caucasian rugs exhibit such strong Persian influence as here. This design is a series of variations of the tendril and blossom, and there is a rhythm built up in the repeated curve of the vine that is decidedly Persian. The central stripe, by the way, is accentuated by being on a white background, whereas the other colors are related shades of the madder school.

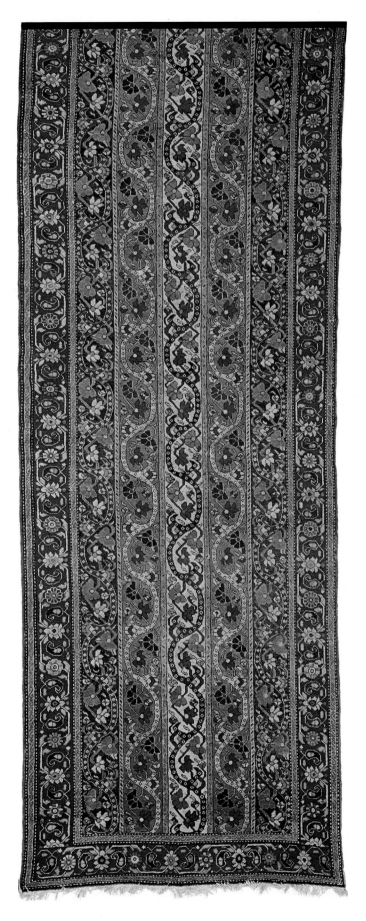

44. KARABAGH KELLEY

early 19th century, 19′1″ × 6′3″ [m. 5.75 × 1.90]
Warp: wool
Weft: wool, two shoots after each row of knots
Knotting: Ghiordes, wool, 80 knots per square inch
[1280 per dm.²]

This *kelley* is again an amazing nineteen feet long but only five feet wide. A hallmark of Karabagh rugs is that one finds every shade of blue-red in them. Often it is used with dark blue or black to diminish its brightness; here the background is dark blue. Another Karabagh characteristic is the use of realistic roses. The roses in this rug are like number paintings instead of the predictable Caucasian geometric stylization. When Russian officers had rugs woven to put in their houses with French-style furniture and twenty-foot hallways, they got them from the Caucasus. Roses were a dominant motif of Aubussons, and in imitation many rose rugs were woven in the Karabagh district. Some of these rugs had bunches of roses on a plain field with no other ornamentation except a few borders. They were produced most abundantly in the middle of the nineteenth century and have a pronounced Aubusson look except for the dark Karabagh red.

This design is typical of the Karabagh with its Persian characteristics. The two identical medallions are common to the region, and the stepped field and hook on the middle medallion are Caucasian. It is the wealth of detail from nature that gives the whole a Persian effect. The little birds are extremely realistic, like the roses; the peacocks flouting their tails are Persian; and the flowers in the medallions are rounded like Persian flowers. The two narrow borders are an interesting running dog, or Sejshour, variation.

The large border has a red background. The pale shades used here are green, pink, yellow, white, gray, brown, and blue.

This group of rugs shows how a particular style may evolve. Here in the southern Caucasus three of the greatest rug traditions—Persian, Caucasian, and French—have met and produced an unusual rug type.

Detail of Plate 44.

45. KAZAK

late 19th century, 7'5" × 6'4" [m. 2.30 × 1.95]
Warp: wool
Weft: wool, two shoots after each row of knots
Knotting: Ghiordes, wool, 64 knots per square inch
[1020 per dm.²]

This is the first of three Kazaks in this collection, and in many ways it is typical of this popular group of rugs. A Kazak has large geometric designs in clear, distinctive colors. Some of them are crowded with detail and others have rather bare fields peopled with tiny figures. The overall impression a true Kazak gives is one of surging energy, not refined delicacy. These pieces are small but strong.

The three medallions are variations of the octagon, a common form throughout the Caucasus. The figure in the middle is similar to the dragon design, and the small "T" border is likewise a Chinese derivative. The colors—red, blue, and white—exemplify the contrasting color found in Kazaks. The crenellated borders (compare the version in Plates 36 and 40) are not uncommon, but the brown and white border is rather unusual, and when it becomes a unit with the white of the outside border it is a prominent and attractive addition. The latchhooks edging the central medallion and on the diamond shapes in the field are a commonplace Kazak detail.

The Kazak area is in the southwest Caucasus alongside the Karabagh and Gendje areas. It is peopled largely by Armenians. All use the Ghiordes knot and favor red, particularly madder, together with green, blue, white, and some yellow. Although Kazaks are noted for their high pile, this is not a uniform characteristic. Some of their more striking designs are various crosses, octagons, crabs, the *lesghi* star, the barber stripe, and simplified *kufic* figures.

Most of the forms are probably descended from seventeenth- and eighteenth-century dragon rugs and Kubas. Rugs from Khotan and Yarkand often had three medallions, and it is possible that nomads from Central Asia took this form to Turkey and then to the Caucasus.

46. KAZAK OR CHELABERD

first half of 19th century, 7'2" × 4'4" [m. 2.22 × 1.35]

Warp: wool
Weft: wool, two shoots after each row of knots
Knotting: Ghiordes, wool, 36 knots per square inch [580 per dm.²]

The Eagle Kazak, or sunburst, is the most popular rug on the Oriental market today. To the Western eye this geometric design is one of the most pleasing and harmonious ever drawn. It conveys grace and a certain lightness as well as the drama and excitement one expects in a hard-edge design. These prized rugs are difficult to find, and at the moment their prices are probably overblown.

The origins of this type and of that in Plate 47 are in dispute. Mr. Schurmann classifies them as Chelaberd Karabaghs, but to the trade as well as the public they are, at least colloquially, Kazaks.

An Eagle Kazak is an unforgettable motif. The basic design is composed of two or three squares laid diagonally across a rectangle twice their size. A St. George's cross is in each square, throwing off stylized tulips at right angles that outline a large square. In the center of the whole is almost always another square of color surrounding another cross. Arrows similar to those in the Chinese wave motifs in Plates 91, 92, and 93 are in its corners. Fundamentally, an "eagle" is a rectangle whose proportions are two or three to one, divided into squares and Pythagorean triangles ($a^2 + b^2 = c^2$). The angles are all multiplied 90 degrees. To repeat an old saw, the impact of the design is due to its simplicity.

This particular Kazak is distinguished by its fine color and the little irregularities in its background and central white square. Others may have half a medallion at the ends or bands separating the main designs.

In the Caucasus there are a number of medallion designs that appear to open out. As a point of comparison, it is interesting to look at Plates 48, 52, 53, 57, 58, and 59. Although they are similar, each is a distinct form.

47. KAZAK OR CHZONDORESK

19th century, 10'2" × 3'7" [m. 3.15 × 1.12]
Warp: wool
Weft: wool, two shoots after each row of knots
Knotting: Ghiordes, wool, 64 knots per square inch
   [1020 per dm.²]

Although these rugs are among the most distinctive in
the Caucasus, their origins are something of a mystery.
There is disagreement over whether the rug is a Kazak,
a Gendje, or a Karabagh, and in this example are
characteristics of all these neighboring regions. Mr.
Schurmann would call it a Chzondoresk Karabagh,
while Raoul Tschebull, a Kazak expert, considers this
group to be from Gendje, which is located between the
Kazak and Karabagh districts. The borders, rosette and
vine, cup and leaf, are used in all three areas. The heavy
pile and rather coarse knotting are typical of Kazaks
and Gendjes, and the treatment of the background, tiny
ornaments dusted like the first snowflakes over a rather
bare field, is Kazak.

   The origin of this rug is an academic question, but
other aspects are obvious. For one thing, these rugs are
always runners. They are red with blue and green
medallions. The medallions are centered by a square
whose edges sprout stylized tulips somewhat like those
in the Kazak sunburst in Plate 46, and they are decorated by cloudbands. The cloudbands are so distinctive
that the rugs are called "Cloudband Kazaks" in the rug
business. The cloudband was originally Chinese, as was
the dragon, and these examples jut out just as awk-
wardly as the old dragon heads, leading one to suspect
that they might have been dragons originally. They
could even be extended latchhooks, a motif common
to the Kazak region. This particular rug has rather Chinese insignia inside the squares in the middle of the
medallions, like the endless knot or a version of a
swastika, a sign of good luck in China.

   As noted earlier, trade led the Chinese to the Caucasus early in recorded history. The chances are that
the most noticeable influence the Chinese had on these
fierce tribes was aesthetic, for the Chinese imagination
produced such attractive and basic designs that they
were stolen by everyone who saw them.

48. KUBA

19th century, 5'2" × 3'6" [m. 1.60 × 1.10]
Warp: wool
Weft: wool, two shoots after each row of knots
Knotting: Ghiordes, wool, 120 knots per square inch
  [1900 per dm.²]

The Kuba district is in the northeast Caucasus on the borders of the Caspian Sea. There are a number of different tribes in the district, all of which produce distinctly patterned rugs. The range of style and color is remarkable in such a limited geographic area, but the techniques used do not vary markedly. As mentioned earlier, the name Kuba Kabistan has been used to denote a variety of styles and tastes but is not a generic name for any rug type. However, there is a town named Kuba where rugs are made; it is the hub of the rug trade for a specific region and serves as a center of distribution.

Kubas have a short pile. The warp lies at an angle like that of the Daghestans, but not at such an extreme angle (here the angle is only 25 to 40 degrees). This makes the rug supple but strong. Another characteristic of Kuba rugs is that the ends are woven in the Sumak stitch with blue wool or cotton, and the protection given the threads by this extra bit of wearing makes the edges look thicker than the rug itself. The three figures are forest green and dark blue bordered in red, beige, and white. The colors in the dark blue field are red, blue, white, yellow, pink, and beige. The outside border is blue, black, and red, while the other has a white background.

This appealing rug is decorated with a plethora of leaves, flowers, swastikas, and jerky white figures on its dark ground. Although the figures are more dissipated than the Chelaberd, Zeiwa, or Kazak sunburst, they are in the same mold. Mr. Schurmann identifies the Lesghian influence in this type by the quiet colors, three rhombs, and the use of green (see Plate 72).

49. KUBA PEREPEDIL

19th century, 5'4" × 4'3" [m. 1.66 × 1.32]
Warp: wool
Weft: wool, two shoots after each row of knots
Knotting: Ghiordes, wool, 132 knots per square inch
  [2100 per dm.²]

50. KUBA PEREPEDIL

19th century, 6'10" × 4'4" [m. 2.12 × 1.34]
Warp: wool
Weft: wool, two shoots after each row of knots
Knotting: Ghiordes, wool, 112 knots per square inch
[1800 per dm.²]

Like the rug in Plate 51, these two are very characteristic of their origin. They invariably have the ram's-horn design through the center of the field and the double key around the edge with the *kufic* letter border. In this case the central field is decorated with birds, which is also typical of this group, and there is often a star border. Although many colors are used in the small figures, the counterpoint in the design comes partly from the dominant contrast of black and white.

The contrast between these two rugs is a perfect example of how much the individual weaver is able to influence the look of a rug made under fairly rigid strictures. While the rug in Plate 49 has distinctive color and beautifully executed figures (the star and birds in particular), the loose charm of the design and gay colors in Plate 50 give it more vitality.

Although Perepedil is north of Kuba, at times the Persian *herati* is seen in its rugs, which are noted for their fine quality.

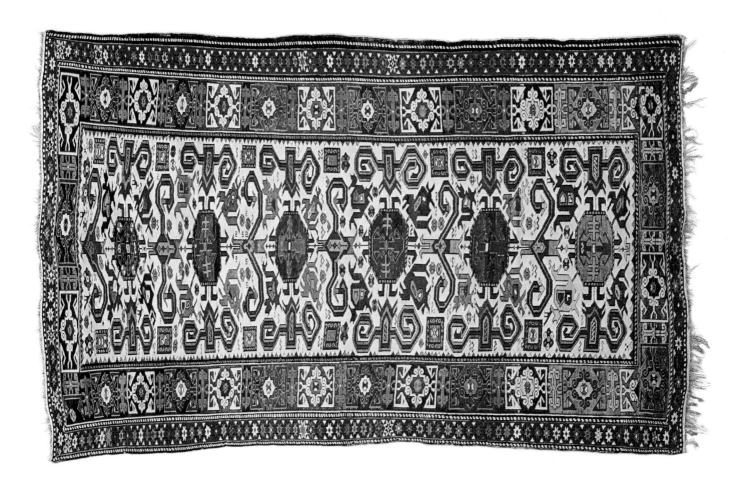

51. KUBA KONAGKAND

19th century, 4′10″ × 4′ [m. 1.48 × 1.24]
Warp: wool
Weft: wool, two shoots after each row of knots
Knotting: Ghiordes, wool, 210 knots per square inch
   [3300 per dm.²]

This is one of the classic Konagkand styles, and it is always made up of the same basic elements. In a blue field is a regular all-over trellis design in white that may be said to intertwine the way a field of arabesques does in a Persian rug. In the "holes" found in any design of this nature are flowers and other small bits of design in any number of colors. Some of the white trellis is marked with black.

The main border is designed from white *kufic* letters on red and is seen again in Plate 49. The letters have been stylized so many times that they are merely decorative and actually do not say anything. It is evident that these "letters" have been interspersed with stepped polygons similar to those of the Chichi tribe (Plates 61–64).

The two guard borders are typical of Kuba designs in that they are blue and black, like the ones in Plate 62 and several others in the Kuba section. (Konagkand is south of Kuba.) This is a rather old preference and is rarely seen in rugs made after the middle of the nineteenth century.

The interplay of light and dark in this rug is subtle but characteristic. The light colors have a washed effect.

The other type of rug typical of Konagkand has a large stepped rhombus in the middle of the field and a square in each corner.

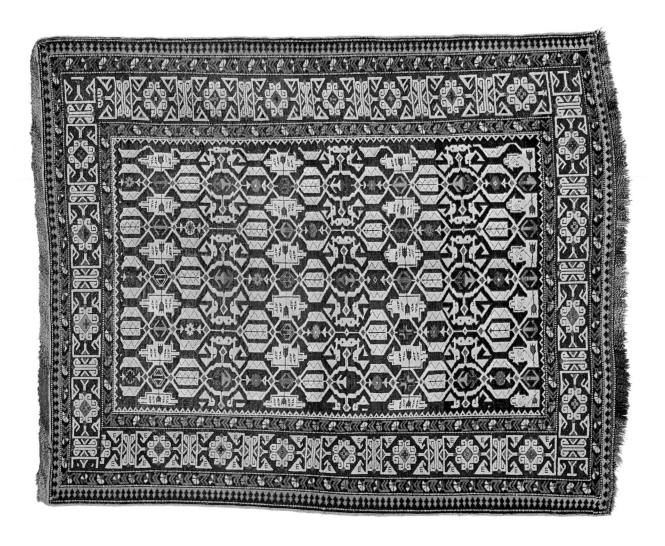

52. KUBA SEJSHOUR

19th century, 4'10" × 3'4" [m. 1.50 × 1.04]
Warp: wool
Weft: wool, two shoots after each row of knots
Knotting: Ghiordes, wool, 72 knots per square inch
  [1150 per dm.²]

This unusual yellow rug is the first of several from this very productive area. Sejshour is a northern town in the Kuba area. Its rugs, though fairly diverse, nevertheless carry some identifying insignia in their design. The most memorable of these is the running dog or latch-hook border, often in blue and white, as in Plates 53, 54, 55, and 57. The other regional mark is a pink inner border, as in Plates 54, 55, and 57.

This design is rather interesting. Very often a Caucasian rug motif is a geometric shape that appears to open out because of rays, arrows, the lack of joints, or a background color that makes the figure stand out, like the Eagle Kazak or Chelaberd. This Sejshour is the opposite—a series of enclosed triangles that use the borders as well as the linear design down the middle of the rug as sides of the triangle. The middle line is a series of crabs and crosses, and the field is decorated with rosettes, but it could also be stars, tulips, or other familiar designs.

The marvelous aspect of this rug is its yellow background, for white, green, and blue are the most often seen ground colors in a Sejshour. Although it was made in the nineteenth century, this piece is in remarkable condition. Not only is yellow hard to keep bright, but it is one of the fastest natural dyes to fade. It was often made from pomegranate rind, but judging from its good state of preservation and from the color itself, this rug must have been colored by saffron or curry.

Sejshour rugs are particularly pleasing because the pile is high and soft. They are highly sought after by European collectors both in the geometric and in the floral pattern of French influence.

53. KUBA SEJSHOUR

early 19th century, 8'9" × 4'4" [m. 2.72 × 1.35]
Warp: wool
Weft: wool, two shoots after each row of knots
Knotting: Ghiordes, wool, 90 knots per square inch
  [1450 per dm.²]

Like those of the Eagle Kazak in Plate 46, these medallions are based on the diamond, the rectangle, and the St. George's cross—but this is probably an earlier development than the more refined Kazak motif. In this respect this rug is similar to the Sejshour in Plate 58. The design is multicolored on a black background. The medallions are rayed in pink or white, consecutively, and their centers are green, blue, yellow, and red; these colors are repeated in the field decorations.

The inside border is primarily red, decorated by crabs in blue, green, yellow, pink, and white. The outside border is a good example of the antique Sejshour running dog. The design is in dark blue on a white background with incidental touches of red.

54. KUBA SEJSHOUR

19th century, 4'9" × 3'5" [m. 1.47 × 1.06]
Warp: wool
Weft: wool, two shoots after each row of knots
Knotting: Ghiordes, wool, 88 knots per square inch
  [1300 per dm.²]

This piece has the pleasing primitive force of many rugs not woven according to type. Like the rug in Plate 55, it is rather unusual in its black background and noticeable Chinese influence. Sejshour was no closer to China than any of the rest of the Caucasus, but somehow it seems to have been influenced more by Chinese designs. It is also distinguished by the unusually strong blue seen through the design. Like the rug in Plate 52, it has a strong linear design through the center that is composed of butterflies and stylized flowers. The "S" in the squares is a stylization of the Chinese cloudband. The figures in the field are blue, red, white, green, yellow, and pink. The outside border is white and dark blue, while the inside is pink and red, both characteristic.

Although this rug can certainly be called a geometric piece, it is dominated by squares and straight lines rather than angles. It has a somewhat coarse appearance, probably because the pile is so high.

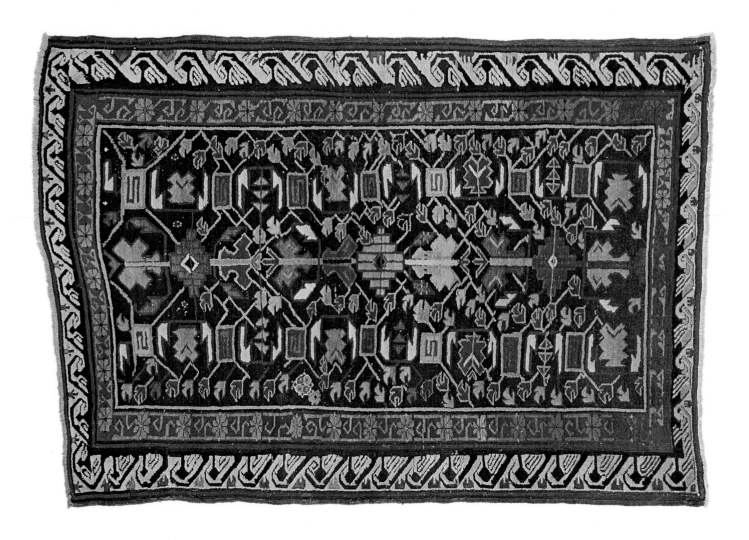

55. KUBA SEJSHOUR RUNNER

19th century, 6'5" × 4'5" [m. 1.96 × 1.36]
Warp: wool
Weft: wool, two shoots after each row of knots
Knotting: Ghiordes, wool, 102 knots per square inch
    [1600 per dm.²]

Although this tightly organized rug is crowded with Chinese symbols, it is redolent of the fresh charm of an English garden print. The colors are exquisite, and the two Sejshour borders as well as the field are striking but delicate. The flowers are red, pale blue, pink, white, and yellow on a dark blue background, and the borders have the same coloration as those in Plate 54.

The rows in the field are made up of bats or butterflies, *botehs*, and flowers. The butterfly is a Chinese symbol for happiness and is here decorated with an arrow, often seen as a finishing touch in Chinese designs. The small "**S**" shape in the background is a stylization of the cloud motif, which is also Chinese. The *boteh*, is, of course, the most popular of Persian designs.

The dark background of this runner is a perfect foil for the intricacies of color it sets off. It is interesting to compare this runner with others in this book, such as those in Plates 42, 43, 44, and 61.

56. KUBA SEJSHOUR

19th century, 5'8" × 3'7" [m. 1.75 × 1.12]
Warp: wool
Weft: wool, two shoots after each row of knots
Knotting: Ghiordes, wool, 64 knots per square inch
[1320 per dm.²]

This rug, which was never meant to be sold, tells a "story" like the hunting scene from Daghestan (Plate 35) and is equally rare. Mountains are in the background and all the barnyard creatures one could wish are in the foreground. In the center are a pot, wineglasses, a horse or steer, very fat ducks, dogs, small birds, and possibly a couple of children. A large dog with a coat or saddle is in the middle of the top part of the rug.

The date reads 1191 *Hegira*, which means it was woven in 1777. This is probably too early a date for this rug, even though it does show signs of hard wear.

Aside from the pastoral details of this rug, the colors were hand done and even now are rich and deep. The decorative details are a hodgepodge of styles. The hooks are like Kazaks; the stepped figures are Chichi; the rayed shapes are found throughout the Caucasus; the "T" shapes in the squares are Chinese; and the outside border is the classic Sejshour.

57. KUBA SEJSHOUR

19th century, 6'8" × 4'11" [m. 2.05 × 1.25]
Warp: wool
Weft: wool, two shoots after each row of knots
Knotting: Ghiordes, wool, 117 knots per square inch
[1800 per dm.²]

This classic Sejshour design is focused by shapes that appear to be almost more like elephant's feet than like true medallions. For example, they are not connected to each other by offshoots, and the solidity of the field is protected by anvil shapes along the border that extend into the field. In fact, it is interesting to compare this with the Soumak in Plate 77, where the central diamond shapes are also stepped, the use of the anvil is prominent, and the rosette is used as a dominant secondary motif. Here one may see dogs, swastikas, clouds, tarantulas, and abundant leaves and flowers.

Although there is a plethora of colors, the dark blue background and generous use of white in the smaller leaf shapes bring this rug together. Shades of red, shades of blue, and a bit of yellow complete the color scheme. Interestingly enough, red is sometimes used as an outline color instead of the traditional black.

The two classic Sejshour borders are seen here: the running dog in blue, white, and red and the flowered band in pink and red.

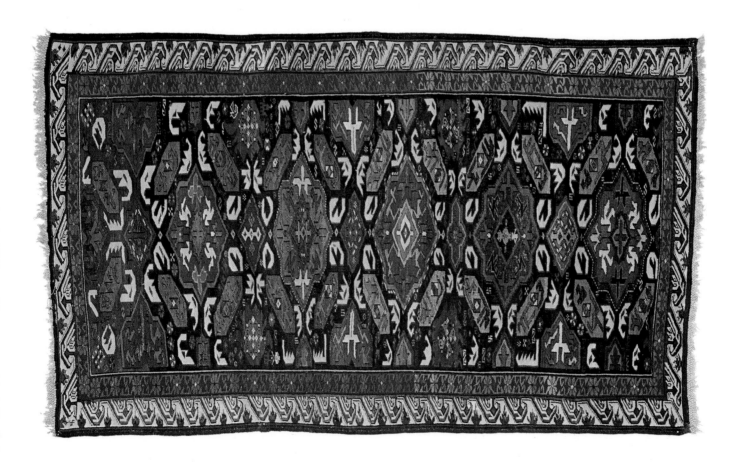

58. KUBA SEJSHOUR

19th century, 4'4" × 2'9" [m. 1.35 × 0.85]
Warp: wool
Weft: wool, two shoots after each row of knots
Knotting: Ghiordes, wool, 66 knots per square inch
[1050 per dm.²]

This vital rug uses watermelon and red on dark blue
for emphasis throughout. These colors, the force of the
design, the irregular village weaving, and the high pile
exemplify the attraction of a hand-woven nomadic rug.
Its very lack of finish displays a zest rare in an urban
artist and brings a reminder of primitive life into the
most civilized dwelling.

Like Plate 53, this Sejshour has medallions that are
similar to those of the Eagle Kazak but are probably
an earlier form. These medallions will later be refined
by squaring the diamond shapes and enclosing the rays
in two more squares echoing the basic shape.

The two outside medallions are rayed in white and
accented in watermelon; the central medallion is almost
all watermelon. Incidental colors are green, red, and
yellow, and the background is dark blue. The three
narrow guard borders are yellow, with a barber stripe
of red and black down the center. The wide inside
border is watermelon with a version of the leaf-and-cup
design, the leaf being red with a white stripe in the
middle. The outside border is red with a suggestion
of the running dog in a tracery of blue.

59. KUBA ZEIWA

19th century, 5'8" × 4'6" [m. 1.76 × 1.40]
Warp: wool
Weft: wool, two shoots after each row of knots
Knotting: Ghiordes, wool, 90 knots per square inch
[1450 per dm.²]

Because of its radial medallions, this rug is a typical Zeiwa product. They are similar to the Chelaberds—Eagle Kazaks, and Lesghi Stars. It is interesting to note that in an area where there is a definite aesthetic focus, like the Caucasus, so many close variations of the same design can be so distinct. The central medallion is primarily white, the other two red; many shades of madder have been used here, as well as blue, green, brown, and black.

In this design there are usually three or four radial medallions on the same rug. Although the colors are often dark, even somber, these medallions alternate red with white, saving the whole from being too dark. Green, which may be seen in the two end medallions, is rather unusual. The sprays decorating the edges are common to all Zeiwa medallions and distinguish them from others. Possibly they are vestigial peacock tails. They certainly serve as attractive decoration for what would otherwise be a dark piece.

This particular rug is beautifully decorated in the field: The stylized cloudbands and other ornaments are rather unusual and highly complementary to the whole. The large border has two lovely stripes of *abrash* in it.

60. KUBA ZEIWA

19th century, 5'7" × 4'5" [m. 1.68 × 1.32]
Warp: wool
Weft: wool, two shoots after each row of knots
Knotting: Ghiordes, wool, 140 knots per square inch
[2250 per dm.²]

In contrast to the one in Plate 59, this rug is an exception to type among Zeiwas. The medallion has changed substantially from the prototype—here the irregular rayed octagon has become almost a rhombus with stepped sides. The rays are no longer an integral part of the octagon but have become appendages. The polygon is a sparsely decorated red, bright enough to draw one's attention rather than colored in many tiny swatches that make up a whole design. This stained-glass effect is characteristic of the Zeiwa radial medallion, and it is one reason that the colors of Zeiwas are thought of as dark. Here the colors are clear and bright. The bottom polygon has been faded quite beautifully by *abrash* into a golden yellow, which is also seen in the borders. Oddly enough, the octagons are separated by stripes similar to those of the inner border. The three dark blue fields are decorated with birds, cloudbands, leaves, and bicolored diamonds.

The wide border could be a simplification of *kufic* lettering, as in Plates 50 and 51, or just a random geometric design. The other borders are the vine, the ancient "S" shape, and stars.

Because of its strong shapes, clear colors, and restrained decoration, this is a particularly attractive Caucasian rug.

61. KUBA CHICHI

19th century, 11'6" × 4'8" [m. 3.55 × 1.44]
Warp: wool
Weft: wool, two shoots after each row of knots
Knotting: Ghiordes, wool, 102 knots per square inch
[1600 per dm.²]

Chichi rugs are easily spotted owing to several distinct
characteristics. The outstanding border, a diagonal
barber pole crossing a chain of rosettes, is almost always used, as are the hooked, stepped octagons that
form the bottom row in this field (see Plate 66).

The designs are crowded on a black field in many
colors—red, blue, white, yellow, and green, all in
varying shades.

62. KUBA CHICHI PRAYER RUG

19th century, 4′6″ × 3′11″ [m. 1.40 × 1.22]
Warp: wool
Weft: wool, two shoots after each row of knots
Knotting: Ghiordes, wool, 120 knots per square inch
  [1900 per dm.²]

Few Chichis were woven for religious purposes; hence, this Chichi prayer rug is most unusual. Although the field is brown, the rug has the *joie de vivre* characteristic of Caucasian products, for the figures woven into it are large, aggressive, and brightly colored reds, blues, yellows, and white. In addition, it has the personal touch of a pair of hands. Surrounding the prayer gable are the stepped polygons so characteristic of the Chichi region. The whole has a rough, attractive look that gives

the design life. The borders are the barber pole and rosette motif one expects in a Chichi rug.

It is easy to see that the *mihrab* in this rug is not the Gothic arch of the rug in Plate 34, nor is it the modified arch seen in Plate 73. Called a prayer gable, it is decorated with three octagons enclosing dragon heads and the "T" design. A candle is in the neck of the gable and hands are on either side of it. The hands are probably meant to indicate where the worshiper should place his hands when using the rug. On the bottom left side of the prayer gable is a comb, and a red comb is under either hand.

Chichis as a rule have a rather short pile but a soft handle. This rug, in its exuberant, showy shape and primitive coarseness, is reminiscent of a Kazak.

63. KUBA CHICHI

19th century, 4'2" × 4'4" [m. 1.30 × 1.34]
Warp: wool
Weft: wool, two shoots after each row of knots
Knotting: Ghiordes, wool, 110 knots per square inch
  [1750 per dm.²]

In contrast to the preceding piece, this one illustrates
how a weaver's individuality shapes and modifies a design according to his or her own personality. This example is crisp and modern compared with its neighbor,
and indeed it was woven more recently.

Throughout this rug the shapes are clean and regular.
The octagons are each enclosed in a separate rectangle.
Bright colors—red, yellow, green, blue, and white—on
the dark blue background accentuate the rug's fine
condition and the clarity of the design.

64. KUBA CHICHI

19th century, 4′7″ × 3′4″ [m. 1.42 × 1.02]
Warp: wool
Weft: wool, two shoots after each row of knots
Knotting: Ghiordes, wool, 80 knots per square inch
[1280 per dm.²]

Like the one in Plate 66, this is a characteristic Chichi rug. It has a blue field filled with the hooked Chichi octagons. The octagons in this rug make an interesting contrast to the ones in Plate 61. Here the hooks and color have been rounded, but the original design can

be seen to be identical. Rather than being decorated by octagons alone, the field in this example is varied by crosses, animals, flowers, stars, and other ornaments in red, blue, yellow, and white. The crosses in the corners are reminiscent of the Tibetan *vajra*. The border is the characteristic Chichi border. This rug has been signed twice across the bottom of the field. Aside from the irregularity of the decoration in the field, the blue in the field is an unusual sky-blue shade. Ordinarily the field is a darker, less attractive blue. This piece is a classic example of the strong individual talent of a weaver who used a common and fairly limited structure, for it is a unique work.

65. MOGHAN

mid-19th century, 5′11″ × 4′ [m. 2.15 × 1.24]
Warp: wool
Weft: wool, four shoots after each row of knots
Knotting: Ghiordes, wool, 63 knots per square inch
[1000 per dm.²]

This rug is one of the most appealing in this collection, for obvious reasons. The human figures, one with a goat and combs, show the weaver with a rare warmth and personality. It comes from the Moghan steppe, which is west and north of the Talish area but still fairly close to Persia. But what a difference in artistic outlook is displayed—no flowery tendrils or rounded medallions here.

The design of this rug is one of the two types from the Moghan area most often seen (all Moghans are rare). The field is invariably cochineal red and decorated with small characters, and the flower borders are so wide as to be almost dominating. In some rugs of this type the borders take over and the red field in the middle is only as wide as a border, but here the field more than holds its own, partly because the two crenellated borders on the outside have the effect of guarding against the flamboyance of the field and the flower border.

The sparse decoration of the field is also seen in Kazaks and Talishes.

66. MOGHAN

19th century, 6'4" × 4'4" [m. 1.95 × 1.35]
Warp: wool
Weft: wool, three shoots after each row of knots
Knotting: Ghiordes, wool, 64 knots per square inch
  [1000 per dm.²]

Following the sparse ornamentation of the rug in
Plate 65, the last thing one would expect to find as
another characteristic type from the same area is a rug
as heavily decorated as this one; yet this is one of the
most characteristic Moghan designs. In this rug one
finds barber pole stripes, stars, and patchwork diamonds
in the spaces between the stepped octagons, but often
there are more stepped octagons that create a honeycomb effect. The star border is a common Caucasian
motif, particularly in the neighboring Talish region
(see Plate 68). The hooks in the octagons are common

to the Kazak region, notably in its prayer rugs, and the
octagons are similar to the Chichi design (see Plate 61).

This type of Moghan rug is noted for the fine use
of contrasting color. Here the weaver has achieved a
harmonious effect by lining up the colors in diagonals,
accenting green, red, and blue with a white lattice.

The rug has been dated twice, at the bottom of the
left border and at the top right border. The date is
1838T (the T stands for *targan*, or "date"). In one
of the small octagons in the lower right quadrant is a
figure in a skirt. It could represent the weaver.

There are several details that make this rug interesting. For one thing, it is possible to see the weave of the
selvages, as the bottom border shows very clearly that
the weft has been wrapped in wool to preserve it. The
edges have been finished in red and white, a nice
decorative touch from this area. Overall, the rug has a
lush quality resulting from its full colors and long pile.

67. TALISH

19th century, 7'9" × 3'5" [m. 2.40 × 1.06]
Warp: wool
Weft: wool, one shoot after each row of knots
Knotting: Ghiordes, wool, 80 knots per square inch
[1280 per dm.²]

This is the first of two rugs from the Talish district. Like this one many Talish rugs are runners with a white middle border distinguished by a rosette and four squares divided by a star. This particular piece is extremely unusual for two reasons: first, the color, and second, the field of these rugs is usually bare, sparsely peopled with small human figures. As a rule, the field of a Talish is blue, or, more rarely, green, but here we see coloring that is unique to the finest old Oriental rugs, those dyed by a master. These colors are so subtle that one would be hard pressed to call them by name. Up close are flecks of many different colors that combine to form the overall color impression. This is true even of the *abrash*. In the field of this rug are four distinct colors: magenta, brown, beige, and peach. There are actually several more, but one would have to study the rug very carefully, almost line by line, to pick them out. By contrast, it is interesting to note that there is an occasional blue in the borders, probably not *abrash* but woven in deliberately for the sake of variety.

This is probably the softest rug in this collection. The delicacy of the color could have been achieved only over time and is a quality one expects more in a Persian rug than in a Caucasian one.

The Talish area is on the Caspian Sea, only kilometers from Ardebil and Tabriz. The knotting of its rugs is relatively fine, and the wool is quite good. The warp and weft are wool, and the ends are finished like those of Kazaks. On the edges a couple of the warp threads are strengthened with wool, but additional short threads are added into the rug as further binding.

19th century, 5'11" × 2'10" [m. 1.82 × 0.88]
Warp: wool
Weft: wool, one shoot after each row of knots
Knotting: Ghiordes, wool, 85 knots per square inch
[1350 per dm.²]

This primitive little prayer rug is naive and fresh. The all-over flower design in the field, which dominates the whole, has the restraint of a Verné but the spontaneous quality that even the most precise French toile somehow manages to retain. The top and bottom rows are made up of the old Persian *botehs.* In rugs from Derbent (Plates 38 and 39) one can see a similar flower design, but there it has an effect of much greater sophistication. The design is more stylized and is used more densely and with greater assurance. The field is a subtle, *abrash*-streaked beige rather than the typical blue or red, and is decorated with flowers in red, blue, white, and green. The borders are blue, red, and white.

The prayer niche has a stylized hanging lamp, and on the sides, instead of the usual candelabra mirroring the niche in a mosque, are a pair of hands. This is sometimes seen in a Caucasian rug (for other treatments of stylized candelabra, see Plates 30 and 62) and could indicate the prayer position. The hands actually are a bit *trompe l'oeil*, as they have the look of a rough candelabra, but hands have always had a place in primitive art. Even though this is a prayer rug, the niche is so high and narrow that this piece retains the proportions of the more characteristic Talish runner.

The star in the wide middle border is one of the most common motifs in the Talish area, to the extent that sometimes the whole field is covered with rows of them.

69. SHIRVAN HEARTH RUG

19th century, 4'8" × 3'8" [m. 1.44 × 1.14]
Warp: wool
Weft: wool, two shoots after each row of knots
Knotting: Ghiordes, wool, 90 knots per square inch
[1450 per dm.²]

Hearth rugs resemble prayer rugs but have an arch or point at both ends. In their native setting, considering the amount of abuse a hearth rug takes, they were probably knotted for the most prosperous members of the tribe. They are comparatively rare, and this rug is in such good condition that it probably was never used as a hearth rug but was made for export. The central motif is on a blue ground; the six-sided figure is red; outside it is brown; and the borders are, working outward, yellow, white, and brown.

It is interesting to note that if it were not for the pointed ends of the red design and the several narrower borders almost all of the widths of this piece would be equal. It could be seen as a rug of borders, for even the leaves on the central blue ground are the same width as the other borders. Because of this regularity the piece is as harmonious as an all-over design. The two multi-colored diamonds in the red field are balanced by two small sheep at one end and two blue *botehs* at the other, which, in turn, have two yellow *botehs* beside them on the brown ground.

The most attractive quality of this rug is its colors. The uninterrupted red design serves as a focus for the blue and brown on either side of it. Many rugs similar to this one have come from Shirvan. The common factors are the red frame as the center and the density of figures overall.

74. SHIRVAN AKSTAFA

19th century, 11'4" × 3'9" [m. 3.50 × 1.16]
Warp: wool
Weft: wool, three shoots after each row of knots
Knotting: Ghiordes, wool, 56 knots per square inch
  [900 per dm.²]

This is one of the most easily recognizable and decorative rugs made in the Caucasus, because birds resembling peacocks with diagonal rayed tails are lined up on either side of the rug. These rugs are usually runners, or at least rectangular, giving the birds a prominent length to strut—after all, the peacock is the royal insignia of Persia. As a rule, there are white figures in these rugs, including one border, and a dark background, here blue. The field is decorated with three stars, which may be squat and not as graceful as these; two are red and the one in the center is white.

The background of this rug is filled with four-legged horned beasts, dogs, octagons, stars, *botehs*, "S" shapes, swastikas, and flowers.

There are four small borders, the inside edge being crenellated. The middle border is white with a handsome "S" on it. Inside is a green and red one, outside a blue one, then a barber stripe.

Like the rug in Plate 70, part of the charm of this rug comes from its fresh, clear, primary colors, and it gives proof once again of the virtue of indigo.

75. SHIRVAN BIDJOV DRAGON RUG

19th century, 4'6" × 3'3" [m. 1.40 × 1.00]
Warp: wool
Weft: wool, two shoots after each row of knots
Knotting: Ghiordes, wool, 116 knots per square inch
[1850 per dm.²]

Like the rugs in Plates 41 and 78, this is a Caucasian dragon rug. Its design is characteristic of Bidjov, having strayed far from the original dragon. The characteristic diagonal lines leading down from the center remain. The field is dark blue and is covered with stars, leaves, stylizations of flowers (many on stalks), and "S" designs. The diagonal motifs are filled with animals and *botehs*, which in some cases are almost like hooks. The flowers are among the most angular and extreme, even for the Caucasus. The background is dark blue, against which is almost every color imaginable—several other blues, yellow, green, pink, red, brown, and white. The inside border is red.

The outside border of this rug is unusual and, partly because of its light colors against a blue background, very attractive. Perhaps, like the dragon, it came from China, for it does bear a certain similarity to the wave motif so common to the borders of pillar rugs (see Plates 91, 92, and 93).

The color contrasts and striking designs make this rug very well suited for modern interiors.

76. SHIRVAN

ca. 1930, 6′6″ × 4′10″ [m. 2.00 × 1.50]
Warp: wool
Weft: cotton, two shoots after each row of knots
Knotting: Ghiordes, wool, 132 knots per square inch
[2100 per dm.²]

Although this rug bears no resemblance to those in Plates 69–75, which come from the same district, it makes quite an interesting comparison to the one in Plate 89, from Agra, India, and to certain Persian rugs. It has fairly muted colors for a Caucasian and is almost totally devoid of the angularity by which most people would recognize a Caucasian rug. In fact, it is filled with Persian *botehs* and covered with an all-over flower design joined by vines and leaves, which is also characteristically Persian. Like the one in Plate 89, the wide border contains the *herati* motif, the other most often used Persian design. If the field were not so crowded, it might even be possible to trace an arabesque as the main design.

Part of the charm of this rug lies in the fact that it is like a Rorschach test, that is, identical on the sides but not on the top and bottom (see Plate 89). From top to bottom it appears to be identical in sections, but not wholly.

The matching guard borders are pretty and delicate, and the central one is fairly prominent. The leaves in the *herati* are rayed. The white outlines of the flower are so long and indolent that they make the flower look like an insect with great feelers.

It is interesting to note that the colors are shades of blue and orange-brown with white and yellow touches, not a combination one would think beautiful in the abstract. This rug has faded the way an Oriental rug should fade, though, and its color is one of its strongest points.

77. SOUMAK

19th century, 7'10" × 6'2" [m. 2.42 × 1.90]
Warp: wool
Weft: wool, one shoot after each row of knots
Knotting: Soumak, flat weave, wool

Aside from the distinctive flat stitch, the whole design of this rug is what makes a Soumak. Each of the borders—running dog, snowflake, running vine, and the narrow inside crenellated edge—is almost always seen in these rugs. The four medallions in the field with diagonal crosses on the edge, the octagons decorating both the medallions and the field, the black outlines, the anvils, and the colors are all typical. The octagons are reminiscent of Turkomen elephant's feet, where they probably originated. Here the background is a rich red, the large medallions blue, the smaller ones yellow, blue, green, white, and pink.

In each of the lozenges are two signs, one rather like the Chinese *shou* and the other similar to the sign for a happy marriage. Next to the bottom medallion is a figure of a man who might be the weaver. The size of the followers circling the field is very unusual.

The borders are much closer to the anvils, and there are no flowers. In this case the flowers serve almost as a wide inner border and appear to make the medallions float on red.

Soumak rugs take their name either from the town of Shemakha or from the weaving technique. They are woven in practically all districts of the Caucasus, in a flat chain stitch that encircles two threads of weft at once and nestles on the diagonal against the next knot. The ends at the back hang loose and long, so the group is easy to recognize. From the front a Soumak looks like a threadbare rug.

Soumak rugs are normally woven of a red-brown and a dark blue, but the early ones, like this one, contained a lot of yellow, white, and red.

Other flat-woven Caucasian rugs are Vernés and Silehs (Plate 79).

78. SOUMAK

mid-19th century, 10'8" × 7'9" [m. 3.30 × 2.40]
Warp: wool
Weft: wool, one shoot after each row of knots
Knotting: Soumak, flat weave, wool

This rug is a Rolls-Royce among Soumaks. The design is one of a kind and as elliptical as it is beautiful. Loosely speaking, the diagonal construction and all-over quality of the design indicate that it is a dragon rug. The field, rather than being filled with dragons, is decorated by stylized flowers, Chinese-derived lattice-work, and endless knots, hooks, arrows, trees, and a few vestigial peacock tails. When one takes a good look, it becomes evident that the rug is not woven in an all-over pattern—just when the diagonal bands should repeat themselves, they stop. The field is brick red, the designs primarily blue, white, and yellow.

The octagons characteristic of Soumaks are seen in the wide border. The design in the middle of the rug could be seen as a family shield. The tiny S's in the field are a stylization of the Chinese cloudband, and indeed certain parts are very like the cloudband motif. The central yellow borders make a good contrast to the terra cotta of the field. When one compares it with the one in Plate 77, it is easy to see the individuality and imagination that make this rug so distinctive.

79. SILEH

19th century, 8'9" × 7'3" [m. 2.72 × 2.24]
Warp: wool
Weft: wool, one shoot after each row
Knotting: flat weave, wool pile

Like Soumaks, Silehs are a flat weave woven in a geometric design. They are always woven in the "**S**" design seen here, usually in two identical pieces sewn together. One dark "**S**" alternates with a light one on a background of dark red or brown tones. Here the background is red, the designs blue and white. The "**S**" shape is bordered by crenellations, and all the spaces are densely filled with various designs.

Oddly enough, this particular "**S**" is a stylization of the dragon. Two feet can be seen at the top of the form and a long shoot at the bottom that could be a whisker. It is interesting to see how far this dragon has come from the Chinese one in Plate 91, or to compare it with the other Caucasian ones in Plates 75 and 41.

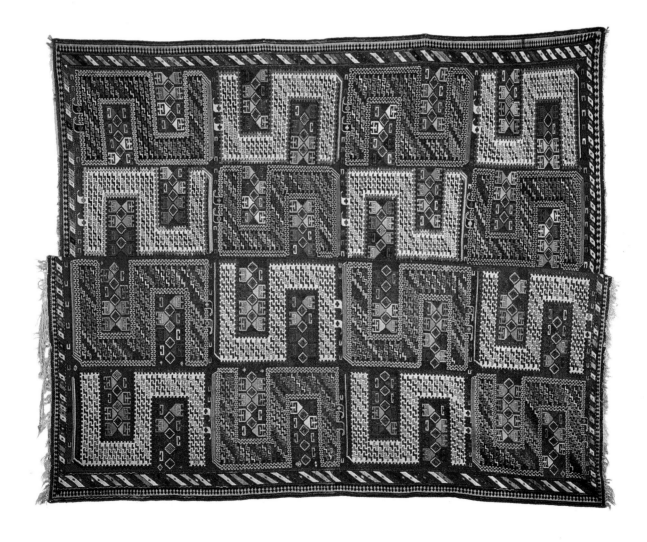

CENTRAL ASIANS, OR TURKOMANS, are members of the Turkic tribes.

They are the weavers of the famous "Bokhara" rugs. Even a beginning collector is familiar with these rugs. Their rows of distinctive turtle-like insignia and heavy dark reds make them easily recognizable, but in fact "Bokhara," like "Hamadan," is a misnomer derived from the town that serves as a marketing conduit rather than from the nearby tribes that actually produce the rugs. The most prominent weavers among the Turkomans are the Ersari, Salors, Saryks, Tekkes, Yomuds, and Afghans.

Each of these tribes has developed a unique approach to the *gul* or "elephant's foot," insignia, although they may seem identical to the casual observer. As in the case of the Turkish prayer rug, part of the appeal of these tribal weavings lies in the versatility of expression found in such a narrow but evidently not confining form.

As a group, the rugs of the Central Asian tribes are the most geometric of any woven in the rug belt. Not only are there no curved lines or arabesques in these patterns, but they are invariably laid out in rows, relying on repetition to create the strength of the design. Furthermore, the *guls*, most of which are octagonal or diamond-shaped, often divided into quadrants of alternating red and white, can be highly complex. As mentioned previously, this group has an affinity to Turkish rugs, coming as they do from related tribes, but they are infinitely more sophisticated in their rigidity. This is all the more surprising because they are woven in such a remote area by weavers living in more primitive conditions than any except some of the Caucasian groups.

In a sense, it is fair to say that these rugs are a triumph of complexity rather than of the simplicity that classicists admire, but it is complexity within a rigid overall structure. Like the Caucasians, they have a highly unusual character—they are immediately recognizable as the product of a wild and undisciplined nomadic people even though they are mathematically perfect, lending dignity to some of the most

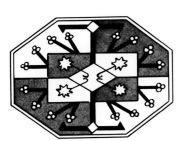

Afghan octagons

civilized rooms in the Western world. The Caucasians suggest their nomadic origins by means of their simple primary colors and equally simple motifs. By contrast, the Turkomans impart their warlike tribal personality in their very subtle mastery of red dyestuffs, madder and henna, producing a wide and fierce palate of reds. The colors are a perfect balance for the boldness of the *guls*; a glance at the plates will confirm that while the red ages to a soft carmine or brown, in the newer examples it is an energetic tone dripping with hostile life.

Central Asia lies east of the Caspian Sea and stretches as far as Western China. Fourteen hundred miles across, it is divided longitudinally by the Oxus River, which feeds into the Aral Sea in the north. It is northwest of Afghanistan, northeast of Persia, south of the Kirghiz Steppe, and includes Bokhara, Samarkand, Tashkent, Kashgai, and Khotan. The last three are included in this chapter as a matter of opinion; they may be regarded as Chinese outposts, but at one time Turkestan did in fact include the entire area. The Kirghiz Steppe was absorbed by Russia during the first half of the last century and southern Turkestan, of more interest as a rug center, during the second half. Curiously enough, they had not been subjugated by the Seljuk, Mongol, or Ottoman Empires, probably because of their ethnic affinities and close physical proximity. The Russian habit of connecting their newly acquired territories by railroad reached Samarkand in 1870 and Bokhara not long afterward. This made the sale of their rugs to Western traders more feasible than it had ever been, yet it was not until 1905 that the first shipment of those rugs arrived in New York.

At this point a word should be said concerning the life of the nomads, because the Russians have forced the tribes to settle on collective farms. The nomads herded sheep, goats, and camels. They lived in *yurts*, straight-sided tents with conical roofs. They could reportedly dismantle or raise the whole structure in a few hours. The rugs were woven by women, whose value as brides depended partially on their talent as weavers—woe to the heavy-fingered girl without a few extra goats or a pretty face for compensation! Since many of the rugs have minor *gul* patterns interspersed with the more important larger *guls*, the pattern might be more difficult to execute than some of the Persian florals, where variation would serve as a guideline.

Most of the antique Turkoman rugs that have made their way into the West were made for utilitarian purposes, to be used as a tent bag face, water bottle cover, door hanging, door frame, or tent band (a long strip that encircled the inside of the tent where the straight sides joined the roof). Possibly because they were in daily use, very few have been preserved, and the real antiques in this group are extremely rare.

But the fragments found at Noin Ula by Sir Aurel Stein, among others, are dated from the third to the sixth centuries, the same period in which the first Turks migrated to Asia Minor. The Turkic peoples were originally denizens of northern Mongolia, along with the Mongols and the Huns. During the early Han Dynasty (206 B.C.–9 A.D.) they were pushed out of Mongolia along with the Huns and Mongols and all three groups are known generically as the Altaic peoples. Some of them settled in the Kirghiz Steppe, others in what could be called Turkoman territory. For centuries groups of these people systematically raided Persia and Turkey. Even so, it is surprising that linguistic historians have found Turks as far east as Bulgaria and Macedonia, from the Baltic to Siberia, in the Nile Delta, southern Israel, and Syria.

The Gozan Tartars of Russia are descended from these early Turks. As often happened in Asian history, the Mongols and Turks commingled in Central Asia. When the Russians finally overwhelmed them, the Tekkes and the Mongols who lived in the east were the last to be subdued (1881).

It has been pointed out that one of the high points of Turkoman history was the choosing of Samarkand by the Mongol Tamerlane as his capital. Tamerlane was the father of Shah Rukh of Persia, who established a school for bookbinding in Herat in the fifteenth century. In miniatures from Herat one may see possible forerunners of Turkoman designs, but it is also possible that the miniatures themselves were offshoots of those designs. In European paintings of the next century are seen non-Turkoman rugs carrying the diamond within an octagon so characteristic of Turkoman weaving. Such designs are found in the works of Memling, Francesco da Marone, and Hans Holbein. There is also a painting from the Middle Ages in the tower church of Assisi depicting Ersari and Yomud motifs.

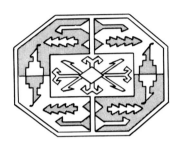

Guls of the Afghan type woven by Ersaris at the south-eastern end of their range

As in the case of Chinese rugs, there are indications that Turkoman tribal rugs did not vary from year to year, and a few standard designs were woven countless times. They did change dramatically with the advent of the Western market and aniline dyes in the 1860s and 1870s. In an effort to broaden their appeal, the rugs were chemically washed to every sheen and color; in fact, an orange version called a "blond Afghan" became very popular, particularly in London. Today they are copied by the thousands in Pakistan, Afghanistan, and India, often in garish pinks and oranges and with a long pile even though the originals are closely cropped. However, even the worst modifications of the Turkomans use the traditional Persian knot.

Some of the most interesting aspects of Oriental rugs are the puzzles they contain that will never be solved. These rows of identical insignia are the only designs of their type in the weaving world, and like the Pasyrik rug, they seem to have meaning in their regularity.

Afghan Turkoman octagon

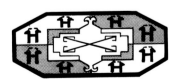

Saryk major *gul*

Ersari field designs

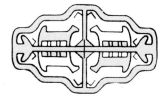

Saryk octagon

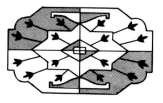

Tekke major *guls*

Salor major *gul*

Yomud *gul*

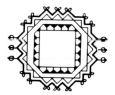

Salor *gul*

Yomud *gul*

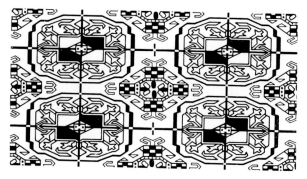

Tekke *guls*

Chodor *gul*

Borders

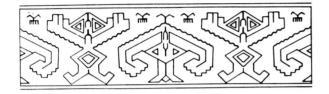

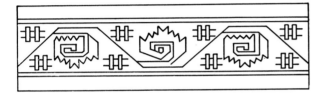

80. BOKHARA/TEKKE

19th century, 8'10" × 6'4" [m. 2.74 × 1.96]
Warp: wool
Weft: wool, two shoots after each row of knots
Knotting: Sehna, wool, 130 knots per square inch
[2100 per dm.²]

Although the rugs of at least six tribes are known as Bokharas—the Tekkes, Saryks, Yomuds, Ersari, Afghans, and Salors—it is probably the Tekke *gul* that is most often identified thus. The Tekkes are the largest of these tribes and their rugs the best known. Their *gul* is the familiar lobed octagon divided into four quarters. Turkoman Tekke rugs have the finest knotting, the most lustrous wools, and the warmest tonalities of red, ranging from oxblood to violet and terra cotta. Here the red is terra cotta. The *guls* are yellow, white, blue, and rose, and these colors are also used elsewhere in the rug.

A few other invariable aspects of this design contribute appreciably to its whole. The rug is divided by black lines intersecting at the heart of each *gul* that block it into a design quite different from the *gul* pattern. The rectangles created by these lines are each centered by the subordinate *gul*, a cruciform diamond in the background. Superficially, the design is on two levels that are made reversible by the black lines.

The large octagon is itself a study in complexity. Filled with tulips or dragon heads, it is divided into alternately colored quarters surrounding a small version of a similar octagon. This, in turn, encloses two more rectangles. As a result, the decorative *guls* also play tricks with perspective.

The central border is a row of octagons filled with hooked crosses. The aprons at the ends are also decorated with stylized flowers similar to those of the Caucasus.

Note also that the "Bokhara" *guls* throughout bear a certain similarity to those in the Baluchistan in Plate 2 from Khorassan. The Baluchi have been so influenced by the Turkoman tribes that their rugs could be classified in this group.

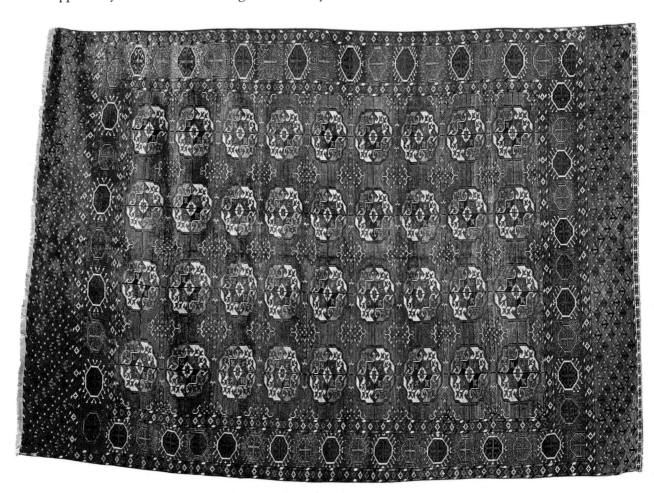

81 and 81A. TEKKE HATCHLI OR PRINCESS BOKHARA

19th century, 5'10" × 4'2" [m. 1.80 × 1.30]
Warp: wool
Weft: wool, two shoots after each row of knots
Knotting: Sehna, wool, 160 knots per square inch [2500 per dm.²]

These two superb prayer rugs are examples of variety within a narrow form. Both are characteristic of the best of their kind, yet subtle differences in color and style give each a distinct personality.

The word *hatchli* comes from *hatchlou*, or "crossed." The *mihrab* is above the cross. Muslims do not attach the importance to this symbol that Christians do, but this wide cross has been thought to represent a heaven in a stylized garden; hence its use in a prayer rug.

This particular rug type has a number of distinctive variations. Some have more than one *mihrab*, probably a Saryk innovation. The Yomuds might lack a *mihrab*

entirely, giving rise to the speculation that those rugs are used as door ornaments. Both are also named *ensi*.

Not all tribes, notably Ersari and Beluchi, made prayer rugs of this type. The Ersari's prayer rugs were more similar to Turkish prayer rugs, the Beluchi's to "meditation" rugs. It is interesting to note the presence of both Turkish and Persian influence in this area.

Some of these prayer rugs have corner loops stitched into them, presumably for the purpose of hanging them on the walls.

In rugs woven before the turn of the century, the rows of candelabra inside each quadrant were thought to be wine cups, and even now a "wine cup rug" is sometimes mentioned. In the rug in Plate 81 the candles are "lit." The really fascinating difference between these two rugs is in the colors—the one in Plate 81 uses pink, yellow, and rust, while the one in Plate 81A uses red and dark orange. Both rely heavily on dark blue, white, and brown. The pink may be silk, and the white is almost always executed in cotton. The wide outside border is similar to a Chinese motif.

82. AFGHAN

19th century, 6'6" × 3'11" [m. 2.00 × 1.22]
Warp: wool
Weft: wool, two shoots after each row of knots
Knotting: Sehna, wool, 90 knots per square inch [1450 per dm.²]

This rare old Afghan has the charm of one whose colors have ripened rather than faded. A rosy brown, almost the color of tea, provides the background for the green and white decoration.

Like the Tekke Hatchlis, this is a prayer rug. Niches may be seen twice: atop the panel that runs up the center of the rug, and where it is intersected by the central lozenge. At the top of each section are three *mihrabs* and three small **T**'s, vestigial crosses.

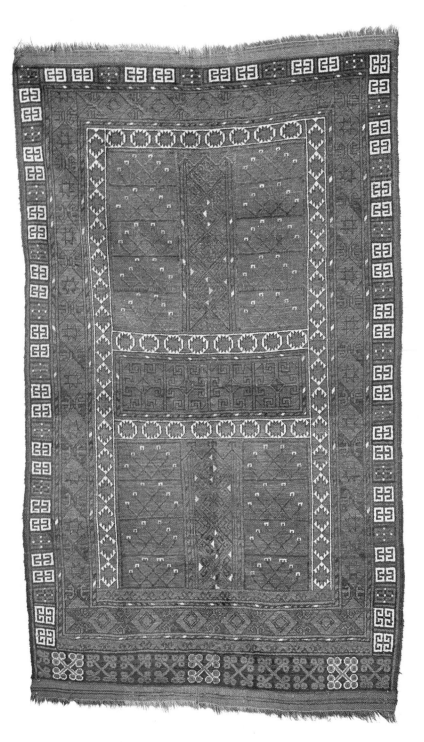

83. YOMUD HATCHLI

19th century, 5'2" × 4'6" [m. 1.60 × 1.40]

Warp: wool

Weft: wool, two shoots after each row of knots

Knotting: Sehna, wool, 128 knots per square inch [2050 per dm.²]

Even in a prayer rug it is possible to see the wildness of Yomud products. This piece is outlined in borders and decorated by a frieze so angular and so dominant that it resembles certain African tribal headdresses. A dark wine red that is almost brown is the primary background color, offset by the more orange "Turkey" red and by yellow, white, green, blue, and brown. The white and yellow markings are particularly effective, outlining jagged edges, triangles, points, and, on the top apron, diagonal rows similar to teeth.

The flowers decorating the main panels are, in contrast to the borders, similar to the "calico" Caucasian flowers in Plates 34, 36, 38, and 39 from Daghestan and Derbent.

84. YOMUD BAG FACE

19th century, 4'2" × 2'6" [m. 1.28 × 0.70]
Warp: wool
Weft: wool, two shoots after each row of knots
Knotting: Sehna, wool, 275 knots per square inch
  [4400 per dm.²]

The Yomuds and the Chodors traveled the desert south of the Aral Sea and east of the Caspian. The Yomud *gul* was often a doubly stepped diamond shape, but the weavers were less held to this design as a convention than the other tribes were to their particular *guls*. They might use a hooked diamond, a *gul* similar to the Chichi motif, or the *gul* in this example, which is similar to the Tekke *gul*.

Actually, the distinctive color in this rug, wine juxtaposed to blood red, is the element that identifies it as Yomud.

A word on bag faces is in order here. They are thought to be the pieces in which a young Turkoman girl showed her weaving expertise and, consequently, her desirability as a wife and a hint of her dowry. Although this is a standard design, these rugs are among the more striking of Turkoman products. They are made with a rectangular field over a wide apron decorated in a small repetitive pattern. The field here is framed by an unusually wide and attractive border. The Yomuds sometimes weave pentagonal bag faces.

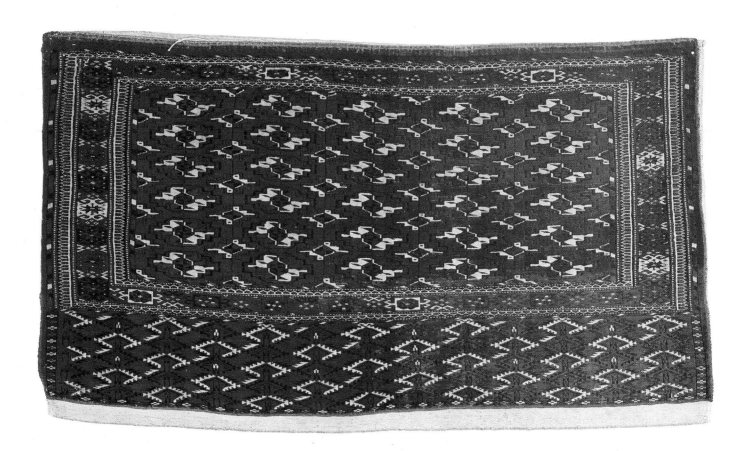

85. YOMUD

19th century, 7'10" × 6'8" [m. 2.43 × 2.05]
Warp: wool
Weft: wool, two shoots after each row of knots
Knotting: Sehna, 88 knots per square inch [1300 per dm.²]

This Yomud is in its own way as classic a Bokhara as the Tekke in Plate 80. It is composed of four rows of *guls* and a background pattern of minor *guls* on a rich red field. This rigidly octagonal *gul* is characterized by eight stylized dogs and what could be two small dragon heads, also seen in Saryk *guls*.

The minor *guls* are unusually decorative, being composed of cruciform as well as small diamond shapes, some scattered, others plain.

The borders are also unusually decorative. The side borders are a variation of the reverse turret with the hook so common to Yomud design, and the end borders again use the hook set off by the same diamond that is used in the field.

It is interesting to note that this rug does not have the black divisional lines characteristic of the Tekkes as seen in Plate 80, nor does it have the yellow and blue of the Tekke's *guls*. These are subtle but effective distinctions. Even though the Tekke *gul* is as visually arresting as the medallion of a medieval shield, the absence of the divisional line in this characteristic rug focuses more attention on the Yomud *gul*.

This Yomud, although not uncommon, has the style of a classic.

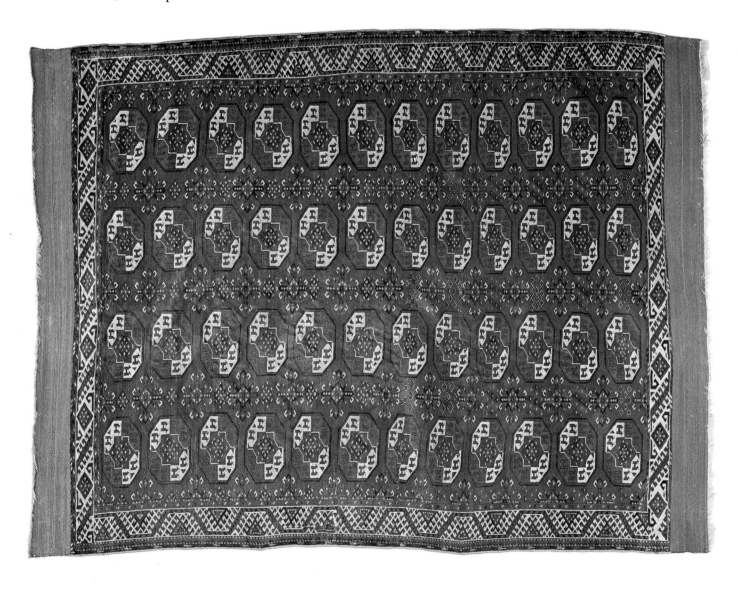

86. SALOR (IN EUROPE, "PENDIK")

19th century, 4'4" × 3'5" [m. 1.35 × 1.06]
Warp: wool
Weft: wool, two shoots after each row of knots
Knotting: Sehna, 187 knots per square inch [3000 per dm.²]

This beautiful Bokhara is made by yet another tribe. Although similar to the Tekke in Plate 80 and the Yomud in Plate 85, the Salor is less rigid and more fluid than either. The emphasized diagonal lines and flattened octagonal shape as well as the subtlety of its background figures contribute to the lightness of the whole. Indeed, the minor *guls* resemble the tracery of a butterfly. The border is wide but delicate.

The Salor *gul* is often distinguished by a border outlined in points, and details of bag faces are sometimes woven in silk. They as well as the other Bokharas are highly prized by German collectors. The colors are terra cotta, blue, and white.

The Salor tribe lived in and around the Merv oasis close to the Saryks until driven out by the Tekkes in 1856. The Salors scattered somewhat, but the Saryks settled near Afghanistan. The Saryk *gul* was sometimes a straight-sided octagon with eight stylized dogs, as in the Yomud in Plate 85, and Saryk prayer rugs were noted for a series of niches across the top rather than the single one seen in Plates 81 and 81A.

This may well be the oldest rug in our Bokhara group; it was probably made in the third quarter of the last century. The combs and variation in the border usually indicate a primitive design.

At one time Bokhara rugs were all finished by a *kilim* on either end, and then they began to be sold (or, more to the point, bought) by the yard, excluding the *kilim* length. The weaving of extensive *kilims* has since diminished. Plates 85 and 87 are also finished at either end by *kilims*. In this example the width of the *kilim* indicates that the rug was not made for the Western market.

87. AFGHAN ERSARI

19th century, 9′5″ + 1′ × 7′6″ [m. 2.85 + 0.30 × 2.30]
Warp: wool
Weft: wool, two shoots after each row
Knotting: Sehna, wool, 64 knots per square inch [1000 per dm.²]

The Afghan is the best-known weave of the Ersari tribe. Possibly because the Ersaris covered such a wide geographic area, Afghan rugs are more varied than those of other Turkoman tribes. They are also larger, many being room-sized.

Coarse and resistant to wear, Afghans share the red background of the Turkoman tribes. They are decorated by two or more rows of large octagonal *guls* with geometric patterns between. The borders, which vary in number from three to five and are never very wide, show a rectilinear geometric pattern.

The Afghan was one of the first rug types subjected to chemical washing to temper the colors. Examine the inner base of the knot. If it shows tones of red, the rug has been chemically washed and is less resistant to wear. If it is yellow all over, the rug is comparatively modern and was knotted for export.

These *guls* present a dramatic contrast to those in Plates 80 and 85. They are much larger, more primitive, and less elegant, but they have an earthy vibrance that the others lack. They are nearly circular and are decorated with flowers rather than angular leaves, tulips, or dogs. The stepped diamonds inside are almost as prominent as the quadrants of the main figure. This design gains in effect by contrasting red, blue, white, and gold.

The color range of Afghans varies distinctly from the Turkoman standard. Madder reds are used here on a blue background, and warm golden yellows—mainly in the borders—contribute to the individuality of these rugs.

The Ersari produced other rug types worth mentioning. The Kisil-Ayak, a related tribe, weave a repetitive geometric pattern using a *gul* with double-headed animals. The most distinctive Ersari, no longer produced, was woven by the Beshir tribe. In it the repetitive geometric pattern gives place to a *herati* field containing one or more medallions—not *guls*.

88. SAMARKAND

19th century, 13'6" × 7'3" [m. 4.20 × 2.25]
Warp: cotton
Weft: cotton, three shoots after each row of knots
Knotting: Sehna, wool, 50 knots per square inch [800 per dm.²]

The production of eastern Turkestan differs greatly from the other rugs of central Asia, but as in the case of the Bokharas several types are grouped under the name of the town through which they are marketed. They come mainly from the vicinities of Kashgar, Khotan, and Yarkand; those from Kashgar are said to be superior. The structure is invariably coarse; the pile wears out easily; and the proportions are often irregular, yet the old Samarkands are appreciated as among the most genuine expressions of the art of rug weaving.

The colors of this region are much more delicate than the reds of western Turkestan. The designs show Chinese influence yet maintain an identity of their own. A frequent pattern contains circular medallions in a field sparsely decorated with chrysanthemums and peonies. Another widely used botanical symbol is the pomegranate, which constitutes the main design when emerging from two vases at the bottom of the rug, spreading its leaves and fruit over the field, or else appears as a secondary decoration in the field.

Chinese symbols such as butterflies or bats may decorate the field as well as spandrels in the four corners. As a rule, three borders enclose the field, the central one containing Chinese fret designs.

The superb color in this example is a result of time and *abrash*. The delicacy of the central medallion suggests Chinese influences, and the outside medallions enclose a version of the Tibetan *vajra* motif. Although similar, the four minor medallions are not identical but, rather, are in pairs. The corner spandrels are taken from Chinese fretwork. The internal border with its yellows and greens is an enchanting variation of the *medachyl* motif; the central border is the leaf and vine; and the outside border is taken from the Chinese wave and sky designs.

89. AGRA, INDIA

19th century, 8'7" × 5'9" [m. 2.65 × 1.80]
Warp: cotton
Weft: cotton, two shoots after each row of knots
Knotting: Sehna, wool, 110 knots per square inch
  [1750 per dm.²]

It is widely believed that Akbar, a member of the Indian Mughal Dynasty who reigned from 1556 to 1605, imported Persian weavers to his workrooms in Herat. In any case, a group of astonishing rugs was produced at that time and during the seventeenth century. Although the designs were largely Persian derivatives, the color scheme was characteristically Indian, employing "hot" or acid colors not seen in any other area. Pink, carmine, turquoise, yellow, and green, ac-

centuated by the use of silk thread, gold, black, and white, added to the luxuriant appeal of these rugs.

The designs were of three types: all-over scrolls; small rows of flowers such as those found in Talish, Shirvan, and Derbent products from the Caucasus; and oddly enough, fantastic as well as naturalistic animals and flowers. In the seventeenth century some of these rugs had up to 2000 knots per square inch.

Unfortunately, modern Indian weaving is known for its copies rather than the continuation of its unique style. Even so, certain rugs, like this Agra, are distinctly Indian. The all-over design on the crowded field is fascinating for its irregularity. It is not identical if folded in half. The borders are used primarily to frame the large Persian *herati*; but the color, lime accentuated by black, is what makes it uniquely Indian.

CHINA

CHINESE RUGS ARE the easiest to identify. It is not surprising that the artistic mentality that created an intricate, flamboyant calligraphy and the most sophisticated porcelain in the world has put an unmistakable stamp on rugs. Their serenity, unique among Oriental rugs, is achieved through simplicity: A minimally worked field in blue and shades of fawn, a round central medallion partially repeated in the corners, and pearl borders or cloudbands could only be Chinese. The usual rectilinear fretwork in a Chinese rug is familiar from Chinese silk and porcelain. It is so notably Chinese to the Western eye that it has been used in the West to simulate a Chinese effect, as in "Chinese" Chippendale. The figures and flowers, on the other hand, are signally realistic. The vine-and-flower border from the Caucasus is so stylized as to be almost unrecognizable as a vine and flower, but in a Chinese rug a lotus is always a lotus and the crane of longevity is always a crane.

Other factors, too, distinguish Chinese rugs. The pile is unusually long and is sometimes cut in such a way as to accentuate the design of the rug. The *yin*-and-*yang* motif in the center, for example, might stand out from the field around it because it is longer by a half-inch of pile.

The Pasyrik rug, which dates from about 500 B.C., was found on the Russian side of the Mongolian border. The Pasyrik rug is a work sufficiently advanced in design and technique to indicate hundreds of years of civilization, and indeed, in China the existence of other artistic media had been recorded centuries before. Bronzes, jade, glazed porcelain, and painting were highly developed 1000 years before the arrival of Marco Polo. In America Ming Dynasty porcelain is coveted, but after all the Ming Dynasty began in 1368, which makes it hardly worth veneration in Chinese terms. For that matter, by all indications the process of rug weaving was not of interest until the seventeenth century and has never achieved the distinction of other Chinese art forms. While rug weaving is an art in the Caucasus, Turkey, and Iran, in China it lacks the versatility, individuality, and craftsmanship

The dual *yin* and *yang* and the eight trigrams of divination

The round *shou*

The long *shou*, meaning long life

The prunus

The three fruits

demonstrated by Chinese work in silk, jade, or ceramics. In general, what constitutes an art as opposed to a craft varies from people to people, from mountain to plain, and the quality of Chinese rug weaving changes from one place to another. While one can gaze at the depths of a blue in a Chinese painting for hours, it is a rare rug that achieves such subtlety.

As in Turkey, Iran, and the Caucasus, some of the best examples of Chinese rugs were made for religious use. The most decorative and charming rugs were woven to cover pillars in Buddhist temples on religious days and festive occasions. They are worked with circular designs to revolve around the pillars, usually a dragon but occasionally a nature frieze.

Chinese rugs that come on the market in Western Europe or America are almost never ones that have been or ever would be used in China. The Chinese use rugs to cover furniture or altars and to scatter on the floor. They are not arranged in groups or made to be used together, as they are in Persia. As a rule, they vary from small and squarish (e.g., 3′ × 3′ mats, once used as cushion covers) to the equivalent of a Persian *sedjadé* (approximately 6′ × 4′) and the pillar rug (7′ × 4½′). Many of our Middle Eastern rugs were found in homes and bought from the families that used and perhaps wove them, but this is not true of China, where weaving is not a popular household craft. In fact, the Chinese rug industry took a great leap forward when Westerners began to buy their products.

Chinese rugs pose an unusually difficult problem of dating because of the Chinese attitude toward copying. A popular design is copied many times down to the last detail, including date, signature, and number of knots per square inch, and the piece would be considered improperly copied without these details. It is also true that, in contrast to the rugs from other countries that we have examined, Chinese rug styles and techniques hardly differ from province to province, so that identification by origin is irrelevant. It is rather fascinating to consider that in a country the size of China there were no regional differences in style.

One of the interesting things about Chinese rugs, but possibly limiting to the weaver, is that the decorative elements are largely composed of a rigid symbolic alphabet that is specific, highly developed, and while attractive, inflexible. Many of the symbols come from Confucianism, Taoism, and Buddhism, but there are just as many repeated in all the artistic media that are as familiar to a Chinese artist as a clock was to de Chirico. Although it is not necessary to know what any of these symbols mean, it does lend a certain charm to know that you are walking over the emperor when you tread on a dragon. The imperial dragon has five claws, that of a lesser noble fewer. He also has a great many scales, an expressive face, and two virile whiskers. This dragon is probably the original of the dragon in the Caucasian rugs and the one depicted in some of the earliest Iranian rugs. The phoenix, symbol of the empress, has also traveled to other parts of the world, but she is executed most gracefully in China. She is a creature with a cock's head, wings, a scaly body, and a long, feathery tail. As befits an empress, the phoenix signifies benevolence and goodness. The phoenix and dragon are frequently shown as a stylization of the *yin* and *yang*, among the oldest

Chinese symbols. The *yin* and *yang* were thought to represent the attraction between men and women, but the *I Ching* makes it clear that they stand for the idea that in every positive force there are some negative aspects. The relationship between the two meanings is probably more amusing than either of the interpretations alone.

One group of Chinese symbols that is rather piquant to Westerners is the series of rebuses. In Chinese, certain words are pronounced like written characters that have altogether different meanings, and as symbols they are used interchangeably. For example, "prosperity" is pronounced like the character for "bat," and as a consequence bats are depicted throughout Chinese art. Fu dogs are happiness. A stag is riches, the butterfly longevity, the fish abundance.

Other symbols are exactly as they appear. A coin, which is often seen, means simply "money." It is usually a representation of the old perforated Chinese coin incorporated into an all-over design interspersed with dice.

Rebuses are as common to the Chinese as certain other symbols, for example, the *shou*, which symbolizes long life. The *shou* appears alone in the field or raised or lowered in the pile. The prunus blossom or plum, the white sprig so familiar on the blue ginger jars and the precursor of the German blue onion china, signifies spring, just as the lotus, symbol of Buddha, signifies summer. The narcissus indicates spring and the chrysanthemum autumn. These flowers, along with the peach and fragrant flowers of Buddha, are the most common floral designs. The peach, symbol of long life, is often coupled with the pomegranate (happiness) and the fragrant fingers of Buddha (prolificacy). (The fragrant fingers of Buddha are a citrus fruit like a grapefruit that divides in the middle and grows rather long, plump tubes in the cleft.) Like the crane, the peach, and the stork, the butterfly signifies great age, showing that the Chinese are as preoccupied with immortality as every other civilization. The whiskers of a dragon signify virility, but similar appendages on bats and butterflies are feelers.

Certain geometric designs are used repeatedly as borders to frame the field. The swastika, a sign of luck, is varied by being woven on a diagonal, between double lines, or hidden in larger forms. The "T" pattern, another standard border, is either connected by a continuous line at the bottom or varied by alternately reversing the direction of the T's cross. The recurring line, similar to the Greek key, is found in all early cultures and is often used as a border device. One simple but effective look is called the pearl border because single "pearls" spaced at regular intervals are worked on a dark strip.

Various religious influences have contributed substantially to Chinese art. Although the worship of ancestors and belief in the sanctity of the family were universal, there were several religions as well. At a family altar it would not be uncommon to see artifacts of more than one tenet, and after the nineteenth century these included Christianity. In the rugs one sometimes finds mixed symbols side by side. Confucius taught the Chinese to venerate the forces of heaven, earth, and nature, and from this teaching evolved the many cloud designs as well as fire, lightning, water, and mountains. The teachings of Confucius, essentially conservative, have had a tremendous effect on

The "T" pattern

The key pattern

The pearl border

The cloud design

The sea wave border

The lotus flower

The pilgrim's staff and gourd

The fan

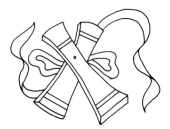

The castanets

The flower basket

the Chinese outlook. Restraint, the family, discretion, wisdom, and above all, the values of education are stressed, as symbolised by books, chessboards, pen and ink, and scrolls.

During the time that Confucius was alive, Lao-tze was developing his quite different, and more materialistic, ideas, later known as Taoism. According to his teachings, there were eight guardian spirits, the immortal genii, who could revive the souls of the dead with their fans. They carried swords of supernatural power, a magic pilgrim's staff and gourd, bamboo castanets, a bamboo tube and rod, the lotus flower, and a flute.

In the second century B.C. Buddhism came to China from India in its most sensual form but was transformed by the characteristic Chinese restraint and perspective. Again there are eight symbols: the wheel of laws, the conch shell, the umbrella, the vase, the canopy, the lotus flower, the endless knot, and two fish. The loon, which appears regularly in the rugs, is the defender of the law and of buildings sacred to Buddha.

Other traditional Chinese symbols are the eight precious things, part of the hundred antiques: the pearl, the coin, the rhombus, the pair of books, the painting, stone of jade, the pair of rhinoceros horn cups, and the artemisia leaf. The four fine arts are represented by the harp, chessboard, book, and painting. The sceptre wrapped in fillets represents the gods and is called the *ju'i li* sceptre.

Chinese history has been recorded since the Hsia Dynasty in 2205 B.C., but there is no mention of their rugs, or any existing fragments, until the thirteenth century A.D. Although the supreme Chinese tradition of woven silk fabrics dates from well before 1000 B.C., it was only with the Mongolian invasion of 1279 A.D. that the technique of pile knotting was introduced into the country. During the Ming Dynasty (1368–1644) many of the design forms we still see today were introduced. The lotus, peony, dragon, swastika, vine borders, bat-and-swastika motif, and lattice design have shown little variation since that time.

The Ch'ing Dynasty (1644–1912) is generally thought to have produced the finest rugs made in China. During the reign of K'ang Hsi, the second emperor, all the arts were encouraged. Floral designs in rugs were freer and more dynamic than formerly, the color range expanded from the early limitations of blue and brown to include reds and yellows, and the use of medallions increased. For the first time rugs were woven in panels, like screens.

The style that emerged during the reign of K'ang Hsi's grandson, Ch'ien Lung, was lusher but more delicate. The colors were subtle, the patterns graceful, and flowers were scattered everywhere, even into the border. The pearl border was often seen, and from that time on animal rugs, fey and primitive in any culture, were often woven. Unicorns, stags, fu dogs, cranes, storks, geese, and dragons were included. In our examples we concentrate on late-Ch'ing-period rugs, that is, the nineteenth- and early-twentieth-century specimens that still appear on the antiques market.

In 1856 the Treaties of Tientsin were signed with England, France, and several other European countries. They more or less forced the Chinese to legalize the sale of opium. This indirectly had the effect of opening China to world trade, and one of the results was to change the character of Chinese rugs. They had been woven on double or more wefts, coarse by Western standards, but since that time have been made on a single weft and knotted more finely. The Western market craved "very Chinese" art objects, and consequently the Chinese made for export purposes rugs representing temples, cranes, and the *shou*. The pile of a Chinese rug had been a quarter of an inch thick, but by the mid-1920s, in response to the market, it was clipped at three-quarters of an inch. By the Thirties it was an inch thick, but now it is only about three-eighths of an inch thick. In the Thirties a harsh process of washing was initiated that is still practiced in a limited way. Chinese rugs are made with the Persian knot, and since 1930 chemical dyes have been used almost exclusively. While in other Oriental rugs the *abrash* is mostly accidental, Chinese rugs are sometimes deliberately streaked. With the exception of a few silk ones, the pile is wool from Cashmere sheep or goats or camel or yak, with a constant quality: The older, the lighter, the softer, the more brilliant. The quality of antique wool was better than that of modern wool because it was hand woven, and the knot ends of an old rug would untwist to give the appearance of being very finely woven. Later, when machine spun, the wool took on a much coarser appearance.

The Chinese have two methods of cutting their rugs to delineate the pattern. A rug that is to be embossed is woven on two levels, the lower cut shorter than the pattern, or vice versa. After the rug is finished, the cutting is further refined. An incised rug is knotted on one level, but knots in the pattern are cut at a slant. The pattern is not raised, only accentuated. These techniques have been employed for centuries, although it is impossible to specify their beginnings.

During the Ming and Ch'ing Dynasties, the production centers were Ningsia, Pao-t'ou, Kalgan, Chi-nan-fu, and T'as-yuan-fu. Peking and its port Tientsin were

The sword

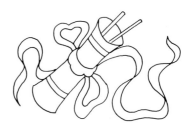

The tube and rods

The flute

Eight Buddhist emblems of happy augury

The wheel of laws

The conch shell

The state umbrella

The covered vase

The canopy

The lotus flower

The endless knot

The pair of fishes

The pearl

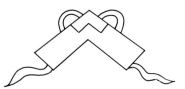

The coin

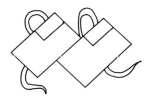

The musical stone of jade

The books

not only important rug-weaving centers but also a natural marketplace for inland production. Ningsia has become the trade name for a good rug, and at times rugs are attributed to that city that were not actually made there. Most of these specimens come under the classification of Peking, while Mongol, Tientsin, or Tibetan would identify the coarser production. Peking is still the most prolific rug center. Mongolian and Tibetan rugs are generally made of thick, rough wool in comparatively crude colors. Mongolians are often in red, Tibetans in brown and blue. Of course, some of the older pieces are magnificent, but very few. The distinctive Tibetan *vajra* symbol (see Plate 89), sometimes woven in an all-over pattern to achieve a honeycomb effect, easily identifies a rug as Tibetan.

In the past forty years many Chinese rugs have been made from designs based on Aubusson motifs, the very French, very delicate white- and pink-flowered rugs that are the perfect complement to eighteenth-century French furniture. But even with such a strong French direction the rugs are noticeably Chinese. They are clipped according to the flower medallions in the field, which is sparser than the French would have it, and sometimes an angularity creeps into the border or the blue is unusually predominant. Given the striking quality of the Chinese-French look, the most important thing for the buyer to keep in mind is whether or not he or she likes it.

Once again a vogue for "things Chinese" has caught the imagination of fashion. A periodic political exchange is taking place between the West and the East, and this acts as a buying signal for the West. American rug trade with China has been restricted since 1953, but nevertheless U.S. markets receive Chinese rugs through certain European conduits. As in every other weaving area, the quality of the modern rugs is less than that of the older ones in terms of color, design, and strength.

The rhombus   The painting

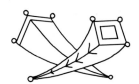

The rhinoceros horn cups

The artemisia leaf

The four fine arts

The harp   The books

The sceptre, writing brush,
and uncoined silver, symbols
of success

The chessboard   The paintings

90. CHINESE CUSHION COVER

18th century, round, diameter 2'7" [m. 0.78]
Warp: cotton
Weft: cotton, two shoots after each row of knots
Knotting: Sehna, silk, 56 knots per square inch [900 per dm.²]

A cushion cover of this type is difficult to find today—it is an eighteenth-century work knotted entirely of silk. In all, it covers about five square feet. It is a depiction of the *yin*-and-*yang* motif on a natural ground with borders of mountains and foam.

The clear colors of this rug are partly attributable to the fact that it is woven of silk, which provides a brilliance that wool cannot achieve. The design is made even more distinct by the ground which is cut down to the knots. While embossing is usually employed to emphasize the design, in this case it creates a contrast between the fresh colors and the severe ground.

91. CHINESE PILLAR RUGS, PAIR

19th century, both 7'5" × 2'11" [m. 2.29 × 0.90]
Warp: cotton
Weft: cotton, two shoots after each row of knots
Knotting: Sehna, wool, 36 knots per square inch [570 per dm.²]

In China many things are made in pairs; indeed, it is customary when buying almost anything to ask where the mate is. As a result, most pillar rugs come in pairs, but almost always have been split up. In this pair each rug stands alone as a design. They are nearly identical, but the dragons face each other on the pillars. The background is dark blue and the design white and biege.

At the bottom of these rugs is another treatment of the waves-and-mountains motif. The little dots above the waves indicate spray, and the snail-like designs are foam. Because the water is level on top it is calm; if it were in points it would be stormy.

Beside the dragon's claws are clouds, and next to his tail is a canopy, a Buddhist symbol. Behind his ears is the wheel of laws. In front of his claws is a vase, and the pearl of perfection, emitting rays of fire, is before his nose. These are all Buddhist symbols, but the wave-and-foam design was originally Confucian. Such a mixture of symbols is seen in every culture in which there has been a succession of religious beliefs.

The top border is characteristic of pillar rugs. The bottom layer is composed of hanging tassels. Over that is the pearl border. The outside edge is the "T" border in beige, with blue used to accentuate the design.

The pearl of perfection has been seen since the earliest rugs with dragons. The dragon's five claws denote the imperial dragon. But his face is more inquiring than fierce. Dragon faces almost always have individual expressions, and this pair appears more capricious than man-eating.

Although these rugs are not finely woven, their coarse texture is well suited to the verve and energy in the design.

92. CHINESE PILLAR RUG

19th century, 7′10″ × 4′7″ [m. 2.42 × 1.42]
Warp: cotton
Weft: cotton, two shoots after each row of knots
Knotting: Sehna, wool, 30 knots per square inch [480 per dm.²]

Using only nine shades of three colors (blue, brown, and melon) and white, this weaver has created an unusually decorative rug. Its field includes the eight symbols of Buddha, but its real interest is in its almost flamboyant borders. The central medallion is composed of four lotuses, the symbol of Buddhism, surrounded by leaves and vines. The two lotuses on the sides are blue and white, an example of the Chinese use of *abrash* for effect. Around this medallion are seven of the Buddhist symbols: the endless knot, vase, lotus, wheel of laws, umbrella, conch shell, and canopy (above the canopy is a scale rather than the two fish). All are tied in fillets, the typical treatment of the small representations found throughout Chinese rugs. The four corner medallions in the field are distinguished by the chrysanthemum, tiny swastikas at the four corners (symbol of good luck), and rectilinear lattices. Clouds of several colors dot the field.

The lower border is composed of the wave-and-spray motif. In this case it is so wide and massy compared with the rest of the rug that it tends to dominate, but it is a beautiful example of the decorative possibilities of this motif. The tops of the waves are woven in white, melon, and two colors of beige and two of blue, and the center of the whitecap is a bright melon arrow pointing up against yellow. Although the wave form is such a stylized border, there is a tremendous amount of energy in this example.

The top of the rug, while not as noticeable, is equally decorative. Varicolored tassels hang on colorful chains. Above them the pearl border has been so decorated that each pearl is in three colors, and the top border is a row of simple, but again multicolored, clouds.

93. CHINESE PILLAR RUG

19th century, 7′2″ × 4′3″ [m. 2.22 × 1.36]
Warp: cotton
Weft: cotton, two shoots after each row of knots
Knotting: Sehna, wool, 36 knots per square inch [570 per dm.²]

This pillar rug, the most sophisticated so far, does not have the simplicity or primitive quality of the last two. Its appeal lies rather in its use of contrapuntal and unexpected color contrasts, its deliberate irregularities, and the combination of many disparate pictorial elements to form an overall pattern. The field in this rug is actually quite remarkable in that respect—it conveys the sense of an overall rhythm even though there is no obvious overall design.

A white field with two dragons dancing under the pearl of perfection dominates the rug. The line of their bodies is unusually graceful. Their colors are chocolate brown against blue in squares, like a modern geometric design. They are surrounded by some of the Buddhist symbols: the vase, lotus, wheel of laws, fish, and knot of perfection. The blue and brown combination is repeated many times in the rug. The dragons have wonderful white scales and tail, fire coming from their mouths, whiskers (a sign of virility), and lush streaked manes. Besides the brown and blue, this rug contains both pink and orange, which are used effectively against each other.

Not unexpectedly, at the base of the rug is the wave-and-foam motif. Varicolored clouds are scattered throughout the field. Overhanging the dragons are the tassels so customary in a pillar rug along with festoons of ropes, the pearl border with varicolored pearls, a half-rosette border whose colors match up on the diagonal, and above all a version of the "T" border using several different colors.

94. CHINESE SETTLE RUG

19th century, 7′7″ × 5′ [m. 2.36 × 1.55]
Warp: cotton
Weft: cotton, two shoots after each row of knots
Knotting: Sehna, wool, 90 knots per square inch [1450 per dm.²]

This rare settle rug has certain characteristics common to pillar rugs and a style of drawing more French than Chinese. It is unique, and in this case the odd mixture of elements creates an unusually delicate piece.

It is evident from Plates 91–93 that one of the conventions of pillar rugs, the wave, cloudband, and foam borders woven to join perfectly, has been executed here. The foam is rather beguiling because its tone is so close to that of the background. It stands out mainly because the pile has been cut. The border is the same on both ends. On a pillar rug, because the Chinese did not see things abstractly but in an order conforming to the eye, the border is earth at the bottom and sky at the top. This is one reason to assume that this rug was intended to be wrapped around something horizontal, possibly a tubular cushion or footrest.

The design in the field has no religious meaning. Most pillar rugs, since they were made for use in the temple, carry at least some references to Buddhism. This central medallion is a rosette surrounded by a design that is similar to the marriage insignia, as well as fretwork and four designs resembling beehives.

The field is sparsely decorated. Eight horses roam through grass, all accentuated by the cutting of the pile. The style of the horses is fairly realistic, not stylized or symbolic. A leafless tree stands between the horses and, like the medallion in the center, form a point of organization for the overall design. This rug exemplifies the type of design that appears to be free but on inspection is totally organized.

This is certainly one of the few rugs of its kind in the world. The horses could have been drawn by a Frenchman, and one certainly favors such a theory to explain why this Chinese rug looks so foreign.

95. CHINESE YIN AND YANG

19th century, 7'7" × 4'11" [m. 2.35 × 1.53]
Warp: cotton
Weft: cotton, two shoots after each row of knots
Knotting: Sehna, wool, 81 knots per square inch [1300 per dm.²]

This rug has the style of an aging aristocrat, simple but with a few perfect details. The beiges and blue of the field are colors that only age could have matured, and the rhythmic vine-and-leaf pattern in the blue border is warm, controlled, and eminently well bred.

Decorating the center of the field is a stylization in phoenixes of the old *yin* and *yang*, the Chinese symbol for attraction, sexuality, and opposition. The phoenix symbolizes the empress, or benevolence and goodness. The figures are simple—the corner phoenixes even have worms in their beaks. The *yin* and *yang*, although based on a circle, inevitably has a look of irritation or aggression when first seen because of the way that

circle is divided and accented. Standing alone at one end of the field is a peony.

The borders are outlined by black guard borders that separate them in a regular way from the large, uninterrupted space of the unpatterned field. The narrower of the two is a flower-and-leaf design in blue and white. The wide outside border is interesting—the apexes of the vine, pulsing with life, are accentuated by color changes in the knotting.

One of the oldest Chinese rugs in existence is an eighth-century phoenix Yin and Yang. That rug is made of felt, and, oddly enough, is much more sophisticated than this one. The *yin* and *yang* figures are complex, the field more patterned and free, and the colors less restricted than those used here. Of course, the knotting in this rug gives it a supple quality and fineness that felt could never achieve. It is interesting to note that this classic design, which so beautifully expresses a tension endemic to the human condition, was highly developed over 1000 years ago.

96. CHINESE BLUE

19th century, 11′7″ × 10′1″ [m. 3.50 × 3.05]
Warp: cotton
Weft: cotton, two shoots after each row of knots
Knotting: Sehna, wool, 80 knots per square inch [1300 per dm.²]

This rug, like several that follow (Plates 97, 99, and 100) is a classic example of the simplicity of many Chinese rugs, the serenity lent by the large and relatively undecorated field, and a decidedly Chinese character.

This is a blue rectangle of large dimensions. Such an expanse of blue would be overpowering were it not for the seven small vase designs in it. On the floor they do not attract the eye (though when seen in a book, they do), but they serve to break up that large blue space. As it is, the rug and its color would still dominate the decorating scheme of a room, but quietly.

This type of rug was made in Tientsin, where the nineteenth-century style was marked by a large field decorated with irregular or "random" pictures. It was made for the Western market, so the vase has no Buddhist connotations. It is interesting that the color produced by indigo is so sharp that even the pale blue made from it, as seen in this rug, is not saccharine. In addition to six or seven shades of blue the rug contains black and white. There is a wide blue border as well as a narrow one in a shade different from the blue of the field.

97. CHINESE BLUE

19th century, 12'5" × 9'2" [m. 3.75 × 2.78]
Warp: cotton
Weft: cotton, two shoots after each row of knots
Knotting: Sehna, wool, 84 knots per square inch [1,350 per dm.²]

Like the preceding rug, this is a large rug decorated by a plain blue field. Its simplicity is beautiful, but here the field is completely bare and the borders are important. Although the rug is simple, the weaver put quite a lot into it in terms of symbols.

In each of the four corners is the endless knot, a Buddhist symbol. The knot nestles into an abstraction of the bat, the happiness rebus, and the two borders outside the field use the bat as a unifying motif. The narrow inside border is a combination of bats and clouds. Some of the bats carry an insignia word on their backs, possibly the signature of the weaver or the name of the person for whom the rug was woven. This border is outlined by the faintest colored markings in a fawn just a shade paler than that of the border.

The wide border is a balanced but irregularly designed beige strip composed of the *shou*, symbol of a long life; the bat; and the eight symbols of the natural elements. The natural elements are usually arranged around the *yin*-and-*yang* design. As used here, they represent fire, water, air, and so forth. They are among the oldest symbols we know.

In a nineteenth-century product it is impossible to know if the symbols mean anything or if they are purely decorative. In this case, the blue field would lose its strength without the border. The whole effect has some of the delicacy and fineness of the rug in Plate 95.

This rug is probably a product of Ningsia, an area situated a few hundred miles to the north and west of Peking and known as a center of production for China's finest rugs.

98. CHINESE NINGSIA

19th century, 11'9" × 9'3" [m. 3.60 × 2.80]
Warp: cotton
Weft: cotton, two shoots after each row of knots
Knotting: Sehna, wool, 80 knots per square inch [1300 per dm.²]

This Ningsia (indeed picturesque) is a most unusual brown, even for the Chinese, who have as many browns as the French have words for love. The field is contrasted with three blue borders and decorated with flower sprays. One flower-and-vine motif strays into the field, a nineteenth-century innovation (before then the line of a border was invariably clean). That kind of border was usually accompanied by a more heavily patterned field. The outside border is also brown, giving the blue borders the appearance of floating.

Compared with other browns in the collection, this one is particularly rich and darker than most. It has a lot of red in it, whereas the usual Chinese brown is more tea-colored or tending toward a yellow or even tart brown.

At one time, blue and brown were considered incompatible colors for decorating because they were on the same side of the color wheel. This was also true of blue and green, red and pink, or orange and red. Now ideas have changed, and blue and brown, the classic Chinese colors, are no longer thought to be inharmonious.

99. CHINESE PEKING

19th century, 11'6" × 9'1" [m. 3.52 × 2.75]
Warp: cotton
Weft: cotton, two shoots after each row of knots
Knotting: Sehna, wool, 56 knots per square inch [900 per dm.²]

This rug and the one in Plate 101 are classic Peking rugs (Peking was the nineteenth-century center for fine rugs), and each has been copied many, many times, made for and sold throughout the Western market. This design has a central medallion, repeated in the corners of the field, and several decorative borders. It is a tea color accented by a dark blue border. It has been repeated in many colors and sizes, but the proportions are usually the same and the colors in the same spectrum. Sometimes the background is white or off-white and the decoration in shades of blue, brown, and even yellow, usually with a few black details, as here.

This particular example is unusual because the color is so pleasing and the design is delicate without being insipid. The medallion is edged by four blue butterflies, symbols of happiness, and the corners are balanced by white chrysanthemums and filletted scrolls. The chrysanthemum, one of the most popular Chinese flowers, is a synonym for autumn, and the scroll is derived from the old Confucian tradition of scholarship.

The borders are made of flower-and-vine motifs, the inside using the rosette that is in the center medallion and the outside the lotus and peony, with the chrysanthemum in the corners. Like the designs in the corners of the field, these motifs are very similar to the medallion in the center of the rug.

The most common variations on this design use the hundred antiques, the religious symbols, or the four virtues in place of the scroll, butterfly, and flowers.

100. CHINESE WHITE ON WHITE

19th century, 9'10" × 7'11" [m. 2.98 × 2.45]
Warp: cotton
Weft: cotton, two shoots after each row of knots
Knotting: Sehna, wool, 100 knots per square inch
  [1600 per dm.²]

This rug would be among the most unusual in any collection. It is filled with symbolism of an exotic and elusive nature. While it makes no pretense of simplicity, it is much less complex than many more ornate rugs. White on white can be synonymous with bad taste, but it can also be one of the most effective looks in the world. Although it is very hard to use well, it is matchless when it works.

In the center is a medallion surrounded by bats so delicate that one might not see them at all were it not for their dark eyes. The medallion contains two swastikas (good luck) and bats (happiness). It resembles an ideogram. Here the bat, often a cute rounded thing, is unusual for the irregularity of its wing positions, the design on its back, and the black of its eyes.

The design in the corners repeats the medallion and the bat in two shades of brown, but again the effect is so monochromatic that it is almost on second thought that one notices it. The weaver has relied heavily on embossing to achieve subtlety.

The inside border, outlined in orange, also repeats the medallion-and-bat motif. The bats, which are rounded here, are outlined in orange across their backs. The weaver knew that sometimes a little of a good thing is enough, for the narrow inside border is the only place where orange is used.

The orange contrasts beautifully with the blue of the wide outside border next to it. Between the medallions is white fretwork of the angular Chinese type, finished by the stylized dragon's head. The fretwork is cleverly designed to make it look as though the dragon has two front feet. On the long side borders two brown bats facing each other break up the fretwork.

101. CHINESE PEKING

19th century, 11'5" × 9'1" [m. 3.50 × 2.75]
Warp: cotton
Weft: cotton, two shoots after each row of knots
Knotting: Sehna, wool, 90 knots per square inch [1450 per dm.²]

This is another classic Peking design. Although many Chinese rugs have a medallion or dragon as a focal point, this one has a delicate overall design that is overlaid by and interwoven with another repeated design. The border, an intricate vine-and-leaf motif, provides an attractive contrast to the field.

The field is white, and the designs on it are so finely drawn that one's overall impression is of a white rug. The blue pattern is a derivative of the Chinese cloudbands usually found in borders or with the wave, mountain, and foam designs on pillar rugs. Woven to look as if they are under this are angular black latticework designs, but at certain points the two patterns meet. At

these junctures are found, in the center, two bats of happiness, lotus flowers, and four dragon heads. The dragons have tongues almost too delicate to be seen embossed in the white pile of the rug, and the whole is astonishingly intricate and precise. It is reminiscent of Ch'ien Lung rugs in its freedom of design and rhythm.

The dark blue border forms a sharp contrast to the white of the field. Its black latticework and white vines are reminiscent of the field, integrating it despite the difference in color. The bright orange and putty leaves and the large, brilliant lotuses are lusher than the colors in the field and are highlighted by the dark color they are set against. The dragon heads in the border are also more detailed than the work in the field, but since the border is not particularly wide it does not overpower the rest of the rug.

The tendrils of the blue design in the field and the vine in the border are often seen in Pennsylvania Dutch art, where the effect is homespun and unpretentious. Here the same design is used to achieve a look of great sophistication, elegance, and complexity.

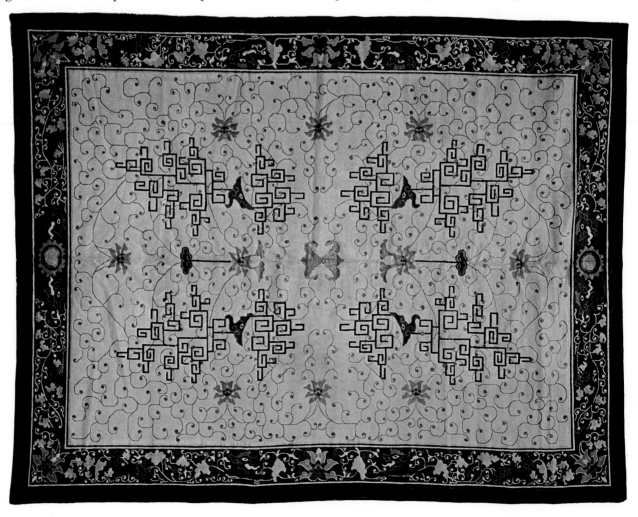

102. CHINESE MULTIPLE MEDALLION

19th century, 9'8" × 7' [m. 2.94 × 2.15]
Warp: cotton
Weft: cotton, two shoots after each row of knots
Knotting: Sehna, wool, 125 knots per square inch
[2000 per dm.²]

This rug is characterized by a pale, delicate design that would be perfect in a room full of fine antique furniture. Like so many large Chinese rugs, it has many characteristically Chinese features but was made for the Western market. Although it gives the impression of being repetitious, the design is irregular, but, like that of the preceding rug, it is an overall design derived from the tradition of Ch'ien Lung in the eighteenth century. It is primarily off-white with blue and black accents.

A series of flower medallions provides the balance in the field, which is surrounded by three traditional borders. In this rug are two whites, putty, a blue, and black. Like the rug in Plate 100, this is an example of the amazing way in which the Chinese use white on white to achieve subtle but effective results. The medallions are composed of white and putty flowers, not perfectly round but a loose design on the white field. The flowers have black stems and black and blue leaves, and the flower sprays show the same combination. Interspersed throughout are putty and white bats, except for two at opposite corners that are blue.

As in several other Chinese rugs, the borders are actually more exciting than the field but, because they are narrow, do not dominate. The inside border is the "T" motif worked so that it is identical turned either way. The corners of the geometric border, always a criterion of workmanship, are almost perfectly worked out. The outside border is composed of the lotus-and-vine motif interspersed with various symbols: the bat, serrated and other coins, the swastika, and even the *shou*, all signs of good things for the owner.

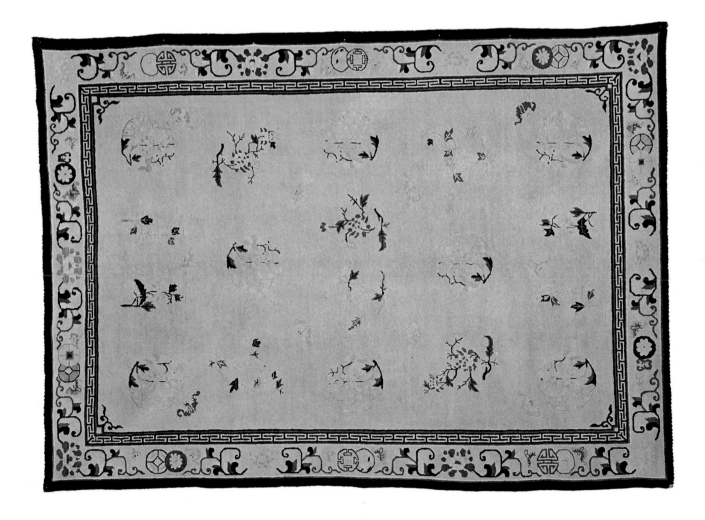

Appendix

GLOSSARY

Abrash A variation of intensity in natural dye that results in uneven colors; often adds to the charm, authenticity, and price of a rug

Arabesque The classic Islamic flower-and-leaf design, characterized by graceful splitting and joining vines often meandering around a central medallion

Baff "Knot" (e.g., *turkbaff*, *farsibaff*, *armenibaff*)

Boteh A common design in the shape of a pear or palmetto used throughout the Orient

Cartouche A design often seen in Turkish prayer rugs or Persian rugs depicting people; a shape containing words

Diaper An overall pattern resembling latticework

Dozar A rug 7 feet long; literally, 2 *sears* (a Persian linear measure equal to 3′6″)

Ghiordes knot The Turkish knot

Gul A repetitive motif in Turkoman rugs, also known as the "elephant's foot"

Hatchli A rug type depicting the cross used in Turkoman prayer; or, an entrance rug

Herati A Persian motif thought to have originated in Herat; usually consists of two curved leaves enclosing a flower at an angle to the edge of the rug

Kellegi ("kelley") A rectangular rug, approximately 16′ × 7′, that forms part of the native antique rug arrangement

Kenareh A runner from 10′ up to 22′ long and 3′ to 4′ wide; part of the native antique rug arrangement

Kilim A flat-woven, double-faced rug

Medachyl A narrow border pattern composed of two identical pointed bands in contrasting colors formed by one line down the middle

Medallion A large central decoration that may serve as the primary decoration of certain rugs; characteristic of Persia; an ornate oval or rounded design in the center of the field

Mian Farsh The central rug in the native antique rug arrangement

Mihrab The niche or arch on a prayer rug simulating the entrance to a mosque

Mina Khani A diamond-shaped Persian design with flowers at the intersections; may be extended to form all-over lattice design; named after an ancient builder

Mordant A chemical that fixes the color of a dye

Saph A prayer rug decorated by more than one *mihrab*; a family prayer rug

Sedjadé A rug slightly smaller than a *dozar*

Sehna knot The Persian knot

Selvedge Threads added to the side of a rug to reinforce it against wear

Sileh   A flat-woven Caucasian rug; two pieces sewed together and decorated with "S" shapes or dragons

Soumak   A flat-woven, single-faced Caucasian rug

Talim   A book read by the foreman to weavers in a factory to direct their knotting; goes through the knot pattern of an entire rug

Tchoval   A saddle bag

Torba   A narrow bag, usually Turkoman, for carrying objects of use in a tent

Turtle   A motif consisting of turtle-shaped blossoms connected by looping vines; often used in a border, where the "turtles" are connected by *herati*

Verné   A flat-woven Caucasian rug with long unclipped threads on the underside

Vastik   A Turkish cushion cover of squarish proportions, not exceeding 2′ × 2′

Wagireh   A cartoon of a rug design; Persian

Warp   The vertical threads attached to the loom that, with the weft, form the underweave for the knots

Weft   The horizontal threads woven between the warp threads

MUSEUM COLLECTIONS

ALL OVER THE WORLD there are splendid museum collections of Oriental rugs that include the most renowned antiques, the archaeological discoveries of the last century, and unusually fine nineteenth-century pieces. Of course, the greatest interest is aroused by fragile relics of the Classical Age (sixteenth century), among which are the following:

1. Animal and floral rug with inscribed medallion, Metropolitan Museum of Art, New York.
2. Tabriz cartouche rug, Metropolitan Museum of Art, New York.
3. Herat animal and floral rug, Metropolitan Museum of Art, New York.
4. Medallion and compartment rug, Textile Museum, Washington, D.C.
5. Vase rug, Textile Museum, Washington, D.C.
6. Ispahan arabesque rug, Corcoran Gallery of Art, Washington, D.C.
7. Moghul hunting rug, Museum of Fine Arts, Boston.
8. Vase rug, Baltimore Museum of Art.
9. Tree and garden rug, Philadelphia Museum of Art.
10. Medallion animal rug, Los Angeles County Museum of Art.
11. Ardebil rug, dated, Victoria and Albert Museum, London.
12. Chelsea rug, Victoria and Albert Museum, London.
13. Rose ground vase rug, Victoria and Albert Museum, London.
14. Hunting rug, Museum of Applied Arts, Vienna.
15. All-over animal and floral rug, Museum of Applied Arts, Vienna.
16. Medallion animal and tree rug, Musée des Arts Décoratifs, Paris.
17. Medallion animal and floral rug, Museo Poldi Pezzoli, Milan.
18. Hunting rug with inscription, dated, Museo Poldi Pezzoli, Milan.

The museums mentioned in the preceding list contain the most extensive Oriental rug collections, but excellent groups are also found in Berlin, Dusseldorf, Hamburg, Moscow, Leningrad, Stockholm, Amsterdam, Brussels, Lisbon, Madrid, Rome, and Florence. In addition, minor museums all over the United States and Europe have quite respectable collections.

BIBLIOGRAPHY

Bean, George E. *Turkey Beyond the Meander: An Archaeological Guide.* London: Ernest Benn; Totowa, N.J.: Rowman and Littlefield, 1971.

Campana, Michele. *Oriental Carpets.* Middlesex: Paul Hamlyn, 1969.

Clark, Hartley. *Bokhara, Turkoman, and Afghan Rugs.* London: John Lane, The Bodley Head.

Clifford, C. R. *The Rug Dictionary,* 2d ed. New York: Clifford and Lawton, 1926.

Curtis, William Eleroy. *Around the Black Sea.* New York: Hodder and Stoughton, 1911.

de Calatchi, Robert. *Oriental Carpets.* Rutland, Vt.: Tuttle, 1967.

Edwards, A. Cecil. *The Persian Carpet.* London: Gerald Duckworth, 1953.

Erdmann, Kurt. *700 Years of Oriental Carpets.* Berkeley: University of California Press, 1970.

Farson, Negley. *The Lost World of the Caucasus.* Garden City, N.Y.: Doubleday, 1958.

Fogg Catalogue (foreword by Joseph V. McMullan; introduction and notes by Christopher Dunham Reed). Cambridge, Mass.: Harvard University, William Hayes Fogg Art Museum, 1966.

Formenton, Fabio. *Oriental Rugs and Carpets.* Milan: McGraw-Hill, 1970.

Franses, Jack. *European and Oriental Rugs for Pleasure and Investment.* New York: Arco, 1970.

Gans-Ruedin, E. *The Connoisseur's Guide to Oriental Carpets.* Rutland, Vt., and Tokyo: Charles E. Tuttle, 1971.

——— *Antique Oriental Carpets.* Tokyo, New York, and San Francisco: Kodansha International, 1975.

Gemiesse, Jane. "Oriental Carpets: A Flying Start" and "From Abrash to Wagireh: An Oriental Rug Dictionary," *New York Magazine* 5, no. 16 (April 17, 1972): 47, 53.

Gurdji, V. *Threads from the Oriental Loom.* John Donchian, 1901.

Hackmack, Adolf. *Chinese Carpets and Rugs,* trans. L. Arnold. Tientsin-Peking: La Librairie Française Tientsin, Peiyang Press, 1924.

Hawley, Walter A. *Oriental Rugs: Antique and Modern.* New York: Dover Publications, 1970.

Hubel, Reinhard G. *The Book of Carpets.* New York: Praeger, 1970.

Jacobsen, Charles. *Facts About Oriental Rugs.* Rochester: Du Bois Press, 1931.

——— *Oriental Rugs: A Complete Guide.* New York: Tuttle, 1962.

Jacoby, Heinrich. *How to Know Oriental Carpets.* New York: Pitman, 1949.

Kendrick, A. F., and Tattersall, C. E. C. *Hand-Woven Carpets: Oriental and European,* 2 vols. London: Benn Bros., 1922.

Landreau, Anthony N., and Pickering, W. R. *From the Bosporus to Samarkand: Flat-Woven Rugs* (foreword by Charles Grant-Ellis). Washington, D.C.: Textile Museum, 1969.

Larson, Knut. *Rugs and Carpets of the Orient.* London: Frederick Warne, 1966.

Leitch, Gordon B. *Chinese Rugs.* New York: Tudor, 1928 (Dodd, Mead).

Lermontov, Mikhail. *A Hero of Our Time,* trans. Vladimir Nabokov with Dmitri Nabokov. Garden City, N.Y.: Doubleday, Anchor Books, 1958.

Lewis, G. Griffin. *The Practical Book of Oriental Rugs.* Philadelphia: Lippincott, 1920.

Lorentz, H. A. *A View of Chinese Rugs from the Seventeenth to the Twentieth Century.* London and Boston: Routledge and Kegan Paul, 1973.

Lukens, Marie G. *Islamic Art: The Metropolitan Museum of Art Guide to the Collections.* New York: Metropolitan Museum of Art, 1965.

McQuade, Walter. "Flying High on Magic Carpets; A Portfolio." *Fortune,* 77 (May 1968): 162–167.

Menges, Karl H. *Turkic Languages and Peoples.* Wiesbaden: Otto Harrassowitz, 1968.

The Metropolitan Museum of Art Bulletin 28, no. 10 (June 1970) and 26, no. 5 (January 1968).

Notes on Islamic Art in Its Historical Setting. New York: The Metropolitan Museum of Art, 1975.

"Oriental Rug Dealer." *The Wall Street Journal,* April 19, 1973.

Pinder-Wilson, Ralph. *Islamic Art.* London: Benn, 1957.

Pope, Arthur Upham. *An Introduction to Persian Art Since the 7th Century A.D.* London: Peter Davies, 1930.

Price, M. Phillips. *A History of Turkey: From Empire to Republic.* London: George Allen and Unwin, 1956.

Raphaelian, H. M. *Rugs of Armenia, Their History and Art* (introduction by Felix Marti-Ibanez, M.D.) New Rochelle, N.Y.: Anatol Sivas, 1960.

Reed, Stanley. *Oriental Rugs and Carpets.* New York: Putnam, 1967.

Rush, Richard H. "Antique Rugs as an Investment." *The Wall Street Transcript,* February 25, 1974, pp. 36,101 and 36,102.

Rush, Richard H., and the Editors of U.S. News and World Report Books. *Investments You Can Live with and Enjoy.* Washington, D.C.: U.S. News and World Report, 1974.

Schlosser, Ignace. *The Book of Rugs Oriental and European.* New York: Bonanza Books, 1968.

Strong, Hilda Arthurs. *A Sketch of Chinese Arts and Crafts.* Peking: China Booksellers, 1926.

The Tiffany Studios Collection of Notable Oriental Rugs. Cambridge, Eng.: The University Press, 1908.

Tolstoy, Leo. *The Cossacks,* trans. with an introduction by Rosemary Edmonds. Aylesbury, Bucks, England: Penguin Books, 1960.

Tredwell, Winifred Reed. *Chinese Art Motives Interpreted.* New York: Putnam, Knickerbocker Press, 1915.

Thacher, Amos Bateman. *Turkoman Rugs.* New York: E. Weyhe, 1940.

Tschebull, Raoul. *Kazak* (introduction by Joseph V. McMullan). New York: Near Eastern Art Research Center, New York Rug Society, 1971.

Turkoman Rugs (foreword by Joseph V. McMullan; introduction and notes by Christopher Dunham Reed). Cambridge, Mass.: Harvard University, William Hayes Fogg Art Museum. 1966.

Wilbur, Daniel Newton. *Iran: Past and Present.* Princeton, N.J.: Princeton University Press, 1948.

INDEX

Page numbers in *italic* indicate illustrations

BLACK SEA

DAGH

TURKEY

•Hereke

•Bursa
Panderma

•Sivas

•Kirsehir

•Mudjur

ASIA MINOR

•Kayseri

•Bergama

•Ghiordes

Smyrna•
•Kula
•Oushak

•Ladik

•Melas

•Konya

•Isparta

YURUK

Makri•
•Anatolia
Karaman•

•Mosul

MEDITERRANEAN
SEA

Peking•
Tientsin•

•Kashgar
•Yarkand

Ningsia•

CHINA

INDIA